ADVANCE PRAISE FOR
RECOVERING FROM UN-NATURAL DISASTERS

"Kraus, Holyan, and Wismer are to be commended for tackling one of the church's most difficult challenges today—how to address violence and trauma. From thoughtful theological reflections to practical examples and skills, this book provides a way forward for congregations and communities affected by tragedy. This is by far the most comprehensive and expertly written book out there on this topic. It is a must-read text that should be on the bookshelf of every pastor and church leader."

—Jamie D. Aten, Founder and Co-director of Humanitarian Disaster Institute at Wheaton College and coauthor of *Disaster Ministry Handbook*

"The human-caused disaster is the most disturbing, most emotionally disruptive of experiences. By blending in personal accounts with a discussion of the many issues raised, this book makes an important contribution to the effort to prepare for such experiences."

—David Boan, Co-director of Humanitarian Disaster Institute at Wheaton College and Director of Humanitarian Advocacy and Service at World Evangelical Alliance

"We live in a world where 'un-natural' disasters are occurring with ever-increasing frequency—Orlando, San Bernardino, the Sandy Hook school shooting, to name just a few. This book is a must-read for faith leaders and community responders. It offers tools and best practices on how to help communities heal after such an event occurs in their community. It reflects on ways that faith and community leaders can 'be present, make space' for healing after such an event. Indeed, it is an invaluable resource in times of 'un-natural' disasters."

—Donna Derr, Executive Director at Church World Service

"The book's soulful insights, drawn from decades of experience and evidence-based interventions, make this text a required companion for anyone of faith beginning or continuing to work with disaster survivors."

—J. Eric Gentry, board-certified expert in traumatic stress and author of *Forward-Facing Trauma Therapy* and *Trauma Practice: Tools for Stabilization and Recovery*

"Written from a disaster-recovery framework and steeped in a theology of lament and *hesed*— *Recovering from Un-Natural Disasters* is the perfect companion for the congregation journeying from violence and trauma toward hope and wisdom."

—Serene Jones, President and Johnston Family Professor for Religion and Democracy at Union Theological Seminary in the City of New York

Recovering from Un-Natural Disasters

A Guide for Pastors and Congregations after Violence and Trauma

Laurie Kraus, David Holyan,
and Bruce Wismer

WESTMINSTER
JOHN KNOX PRESS
LOUISVILLE · KENTUCKY

First edition
Published by Westminster John Knox Press
Louisville, Kentucky

17 18 19 20 21 22 23 24 25 26—10 9 8 7 6 5 4 3 2 1

Scripture quotations from the New Revised Standard Version of the Bible are copyright © 1989 by the Division of Christian Education of the National Council of the Churches of Christ in the U.S.A. and are used by permission.

Scripture quotations marked KJV are from the King James or Authorized Version of the Bible.

"God, We've Known Such Grief and Anger," text © Carolyn Winfrey Gillette, 2002, in *Songs of Grace: New Hymns for God and Neighbor* by Carolyn Winfrey Gillette (Nashville: Upper Room Books, 2009). Used by permission. All rights reserved. Permission to use this hymn is given for local church use. For more disaster (natural and human) related hymns, see www.carolynshymns.com.

Every effort has been made to determine whether texts are under copyright. If through an oversight any copyrighted material has been used without permission, and the publisher is notified of this, acknowledgment will be made in future printings.

Book design by Drew Stevens
Cover design by Barbara LeVan Fisher, www.levanfisherstudio.com
Cover photo by Richard Ellis / Alamy

Library of Congress Cataloging-in-Publication Data

Names: Kraus, Laurie, author. | Holyan, David, author. | Wismer, Bruce, author.
Title: Recovering from un-natural disasters : a guide for pastors and congregations after violence and trauma / Laurie Kraus, David Holyan, and Bruce Wismer.
Description: Louisville, KY : Westminster John Knox Press, [2017] | Includes bibliographical references.
Identifiers: LCCN 2016032996 (print) | LCCN 2016048417 (ebook) | ISBN 9780664262150 (pbk. : alk. paper) | ISBN 9781611647907 (ebook)
Subjects: LCSH: Pastoral psychology. | Psychology, Religious. | Violence--Religious aspects--Christianity. | Suffering--Religious aspects--Christianity. | Psychic trauma--Religious aspects--Christianity. | Post-traumatic stress disorder--Religious aspects--Christianity.
Classification: LCC BV4012 .K69 2017 (print) | LCC BV4012 (ebook) | DDC 253.5/2--dc23
LC record available at https://lccn.loc.gov/2016032996

∞ The paper used in this publication meets the minimum requirements of the American National Standard for Information Sciences—Permanence of Paper for Printed Library Materials, ANSI Z39.48-1992.

Most Westminster John Knox Press books are available at special quantity discounts when purchased in bulk by corporations, organizations, and special-interest groups. For more information, please e-mail SpecialSales@wjkbooks.com.

To the communities of faith who walk with courage
through the valley of the shadow of trauma and violence
bearing light in the midst of darkness, and nourishing hope out of despair

Contents

Appendixes: Worship Resources

Acknowledgments

We would like to acknowledge and thank the Rev. Dr. Kate Wiebe for her contributions to this project and her partnership in this ministry. Also, we are grateful to David Maxwell, our very able editor at Westminster John Knox, "for he is like a refiner's fire." His gift for clarifying language and simplifying our elaborate "preacher-speak" made this book clearer and stronger.

We would like to thank our spouses: Karen, Warren, and Jani. We would also like to thank the beloved people of First Presbyterian Church of Kirkwood, MO, Pine Shores Presbyterian Church in Sarasota, FL, Riviera Presbyterian Church in Miami, FL, and Presbyterian Disaster Assistance, in the ministry area of Compassion, Peace and Justice. Most especially we offer our deep gratitude to the communities of faith that welcomed us in the midst of tragedy, allowing us to walk with them through the valley of the shadow. May they continue to thrive and grow in wisdom.

Introduction

It was very unusual that our church administrator had not come to work that day. Her father-in-law had expressed concern for the whole family, given its history of stress and domestic violence. In the minutes, then hours, that followed, sadly we discovered that our worst fears had become a reality. The doors of the house adjacent to the church where Kathy, her husband, and teenage son resided were bolted shut; each door had a note taped to it instructing the reader to call the police. It was a "double-murder-suicide."

"You have one hour before the public police blotter is updated online," the police chief stated with some concern for us, like he was doing his best to point out that the ocean before us was suddenly receding and a tsunami wave would be descending momentarily. The phones rang incessantly. Investigators, hazardous materials personnel, and prime-time media encamped around the church's grounds.

A disaster. A human-caused disaster. When violence impacts an entire congregation or community, and not just a family or individuals, when its rippling effects spread throughout the local streets or across the land, it is a disaster. This book describes what happens when violent disaster impacts a congregation. It will give you language, examples, and a template for turning pastoral attention to the kind of healing practices that will most help your congregation.

The physical, emotional, and spiritual ripple effects after violence are far-reaching; effects that experts say can even pass through generations when not responded to in healthy ways. They temporarily overwhelm a group's ability to cope and sometimes permanently alter the group's composition. What follows here is a collection of examples, best practices, and hard-learned expertise for practicing resilience and restoring congregations by moving through the devastation of violence toward reforming and wisdom. This book is intended to be an accessible resource for quick reference in the event of a crisis as well as a timely study.

To begin the conversation, it is important to define the concepts of trauma, congregational trauma or disaster, violence, and the valley of the shadow of death—a foundational metaphor for navigating the beginning steps of healing. Trauma occurs when a person or community experiences a painful, threatening, or violent event that disrupts and overwhelms normal functioning. Sometimes, traumatic events that directly impact a person and a family contribute to congregational trauma. Congregational trauma or disaster refers to an event or series of events that temporarily overwhelm and permanently alter the relational structure and environment of a congregation. Such events may be community-wide or occur within the congregation. Violence can be a form of individual or congregational trauma or disaster. Violence is a human-initiated act of assault on another human being, a group, or facilities that results in physical or emotional damage—in some cases, that damage is traumatic. Violent traumas may involve shootings, rape, physical or domestic abuse, arson, bombing, poison, or other forms of destruction.

Responding to violence requires a different focus and set of skills from responding to natural disasters or industrial accidents. Both natural and "un-natural" disasters cause victims to be disoriented, destabilized, and engrossed in chaos. It can seem as if there is no hope and no way out. Though natural disasters and industrial accidents cause great loss and can overwhelm abilities to cope, human-caused violence has an additional component. It forces us to face the wretched and high cost of human frailty, and what many faithful people understand as sin. That is, a tornado that wipes out a neighborhood is traumatic. But a mass shooting or bombing was caused by a human being.

Un-natural disasters force us to reckon with whether love and forgiveness really do conquer all; or if those are just mythical ideals in the face of life-altering realities. The immediate aftermath of violence is a stark and discouraging landscape we refer to as the valley of the shadow of death: a cavern that stands between resurrection and us. The phrase comes from Psalm 23 in the Hebrew and Christian Bible, and in this book, it refers to the personal or communal state of being caught in the abyss that follows traumatic loss. Traversing it successfully requires intentional care and companionship.

Our concern in this book is how churches develop and practice resilience after traumatic violence—that is, how they navigate through and beyond the valley of the shadow. In our experience, this trek requires attending to what theologian Shelly Rambo describes as "what remains"[1] after trauma. In the case of violence and its immediate aftermath, what remains for many congregations are shattered hope, debilitated human spirits, devastated mission, exhausted stewardship, and the immensely strong temptation to avoid the pain, anger, resentment, heartache, and burdens of loss. Though the way out of the dark valley does exist, the journey is neither easy nor quick. The great poet Robert Frost says, "The best way out is always through."[2] The road to healing after violence is through what remains.

THE FAR-REACHING IMPACTS

On May 20, 2007, in Moscow, Idaho, Jason K. Hamilton left the bar where he had been sitting with a friend, went home, and fatally shot his wife. Carrying two semiautomatic rifles, he drove to the county courthouse, where he opened fire on the building, killing one responder and wounding others. He then ran into First Presbyterian Church. After firing many more rounds, he shot and killed the church caretaker and then committed suicide in the sanctuary. Parishioners arrived the next day for worship to find the building wrapped in yellow tape as the scene of a very violent crime.

The word *trauma* comes from the Greek word *troma*, meaning "a wound," "a hurt," "a defeat." When an act of violence afflicts a community of faith, all three definitions have resonance. *How could this happen here?* When sacred space—where people are baptized and married, where the Word is proclaimed and heard, the sanctuary where God can be found—has been violated, the hurt goes deep, deeper than we could have imagined. *How can we ever drop the kids off in that Sunday school room? How will I sit at my desk in that office, without seeing the blood and his body? Can I process into the choir loft and sing God's praises without imagining how the shooter felt, sitting and looking at our beautiful cross as he prepared to end his own life?* How can anyone ever look at the church in the same way again?

The fluttering of police barricade tape that refuses people entrance to their church home and the presence of crime-scene cleanup crews violate the idea of sacred space. Long after the buildings have been returned to church custody, the sight of newly painted walls or refurnished offices and classrooms cause members pain and elicit memory, producing a hurt that may go on for many seasons, affecting the way people and staff participate—or don't participate—in the life of their faith community. The very idea of the holiness of sanctuary, and the refuge of faith upon which so many depend, is challenged by the realities of the violence swirling around it and among its people.

Even when the church building is not the locus of public violence, a sense of defeat often pervades congregations in communities that endure such events. Though it may seem illogical on the surface, the congregation's task of bearing witness to the presence of God and bringing practices of justice, kindness, and mercy to their world is challenged by the eruption of violence and death at the elementary school down the street, the college downtown, the local grocery store, or the movie theater where the youth group went just last Sunday afternoon. Communities of faith are meant to represent the goodness of life, the possibility of divine blessing, the commitment of neighbors to care for one another and sustain their community's well-being. The congregation's implicit covenant with the civic community in which they dwell is broken when a shooter or a bomb destroys that goodness and shatters peace and the ordinary practices of neighborliness. Feelings of shame, a sense of futility, and anger often ensue.

In the turbulent wake of such tragic events, faith communities of all kinds struggle with intensified questions of meaning; struggling to make sense of and reinterpret their mission, ministry, and common life in the aftermath.

A DISASTER TRAJECTORY: HOW WE GOT HERE

The chart below, and others like it, has been in general circulation among disaster response organizations for more than a decade, helping survivors and helpers envision the trajectories of community healing after disaster. But that chart focused on only the elements related to natural disasters. With no model existing for human-caused disaster, we used this model for some of our initial responses to congregational trauma and violence. The chart includes six phases as a guideline: warning/anticipation, impact/emergency/rescue, aftermath/assessment, relief/remedy, short-term recovery and long-term recovery, and reconstruction.

PHASES OF DISASTER

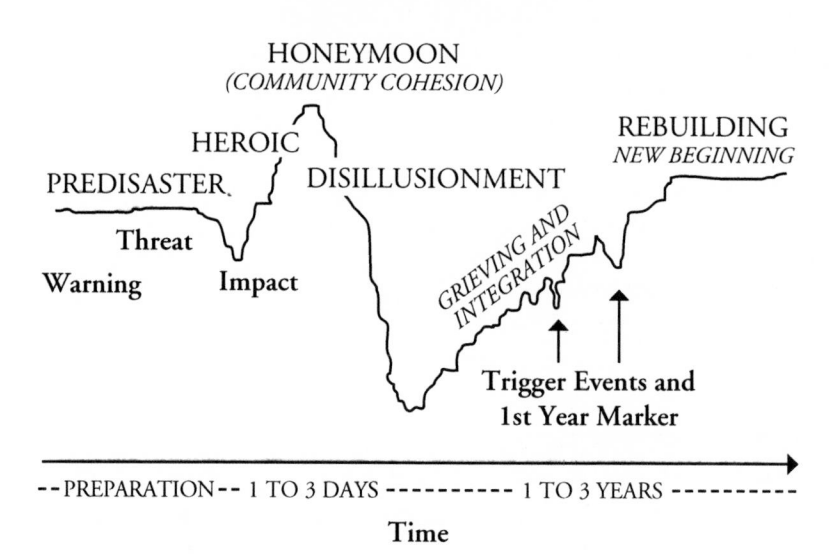

Early responses to human-caused disaster utilized the natural-disaster model as a template, but in time, as responders' experience in congregational trauma expanded and deepened, it became clear that these phases were not completely applicable. New questions focused research and practice on understanding the differences and similarities between natural and un-natural disaster. We were struck by the comments and experience of one pastoral staff group who attended a support and resilience event for pastors who had survived a disaster and recovery process sometime in the past two years. During the social time, as pastors introduced themselves informally to their neighbors, the question naturally arose: "What happened to you?" While those who had experienced natural disaster shared easily and energetically about their experiences and showed interest in the experience of others, all four pastors from a church whose "disaster" had been a double murder and suicide in the church manse were met with stunned silence, followed by an awkward "Oh," that trailed off into silence as the inquirers excused themselves as quickly as possible. One of the pastors later reflected, "We already feel so strange and different since the tragedy . . . we thought that here, with other survivors, we would feel at home, but the violent event makes us so different from the others that we feel like freaks." The natural-disaster model doesn't work for human-caused disaster, so we modified the movements or phases, condensing them into four phases.

THE FOUR PHASES OF HUMAN-CAUSED DISASTER RESPONSE

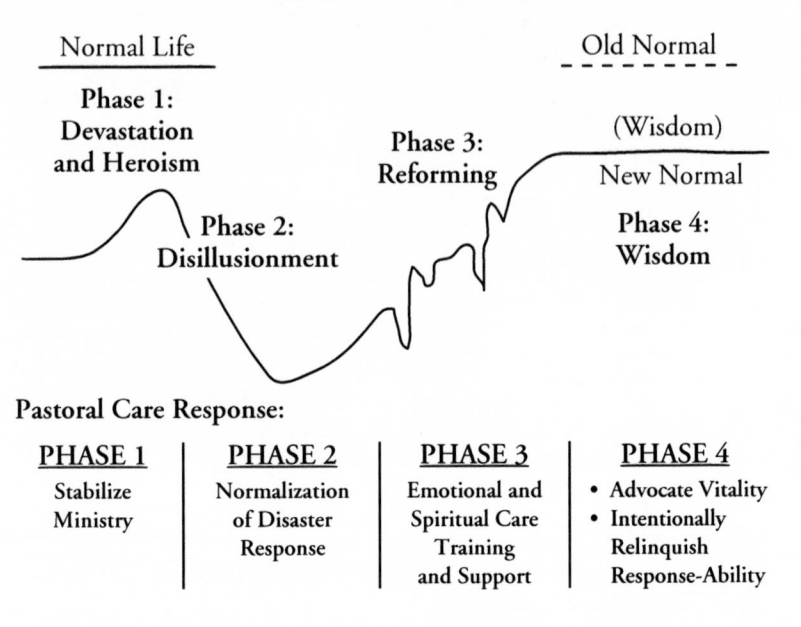

Normal Life

Old Normal

Phase 1:
Devastation
and Heroism

Phase 3:
Reforming

(Wisdom)

New Normal

Phase 2:
Disillusionment

Phase 4:
Wisdom

Pastoral Care Response:

PHASE 1	PHASE 2	PHASE 3	PHASE 4
Stabilize Ministry	Normalization of Disaster Response	Emotional and Spiritual Care Training and Support	• Advocate Vitality • Intentionally Relinquish Response-Ability

Phase One signifies the Devastation and Heroic periods most groups encounter in the aftermath of an un-natural disaster. This phase is followed by a difficult period of Disillusionment, Phase Two. At a critical turn, the timing of which is unique to each congregation, a subtle and gradual upward movement toward healing begins. Phase Three involves the months and years of Reforming, a season of reimagining and rebuilding life together as the trauma becomes an integrated part of the community's narrative. Phase Four shows the congregation and its leaders emerging into a new normal, marked by Wisdom. We believe that the phases and trajectory in this book most accurately describe what congregations commonly experience in the aftermath of a violent incident. These movements reflect the best wisdom that experience has taught us in responding to violence and trauma in a congregation. This book is based on these phases.

CHAPTER OUTLINE

Individual chapters will focus on the four phases and will discuss the key elements of calming, connection, and communicating narrative. Some chapters provide guidance for worship and address theological approaches to violence and trauma. Appendixes following offer sample liturgies, prayers, and sermon ideas and describe for leaders and parents the effects of trauma on children and youth. The phases are described briefly below.

Devastation and Heroism (Phase One)

Violence and trauma are devastating to a congregation. After violence, there is a sense of powerlessness, bewilderment, and shock. Whatever ordinary life the congregation was in the midst of—preparing the newsletter, reviewing the worship calendar, developing the capital campaign, planning for the mission fair—is no longer the business for the day (or for many days ahead). After a traumatic event, stabilization of the ministry is the primary goal. This chapter focuses on the impact of devastation in the faith community and the heroic behaviors of those involved in responding to violence and trauma, how to be a helpful presence in the midst of a congregational trauma, and methods for faith leaders who are involved in responding to take care of themselves.

Disillusionment (Phase Two)

Over time, heroic behavior subsides. Response to trauma demands something more. When finally there is nothing left to rescue, there is no more illusion that heroic energy can fix the loss. After the Devastation and Heroism phase, anger, absence, confusion, denial, and despair accompany the community's disturbing shift into the next phase of the process: Disillusionment. Even though Disillusionment emerges naturally, it is a difficult season and often resisted. The disaster—the trauma—happened. It is as bad as it feels. We cannot go back to the way things were. We are left with the shattering, discouraging, and painful reality that life will never be the same again. There is only a different life forward from the way things used to be, a way forward that is unfamiliar and hidden in shadow.

Disillusionment is perhaps the most complex of the four phases because of the many difficult personal and corporate dynamics involved. The chart shows a sharp decline from the top peak of heroism to the lowest point in the recovery and healing process. Navigating this phase well requires a consistent and less anxious presence, effective communication skills, the capacity to tolerate intense emotions, and a commitment to maintain boundaries. People move through the Disillusionment phase at varying paces and not all at once, challenging the unity of congregational life and process as it drives forward through the valley of the shadow.

Reforming and Wisdom (Phases Three and Four)

After Disillusionment settles, when the grief of the violence and trauma has been individually and collectively lived with and lamented, when the struggle has been integrated and no longer avoided, and when the remnant is stable, the foundation has been established for the hard work of Reforming and moving toward Wisdom. Since violence and trauma prevent anything from being restored to its original condition, this is a time of building up anew, revising, reimagining, and rebuilding. This phase is marked by hope but also by confusion, and is often infused with conflict. It requires intentional commitment to stay together and work together to build up one another and the beloved community again. It is a re-visioning and a rebuilding of purpose and priorities that will lead the community, in due season, to the green pastures and still waters where God is once again recognized and experienced as the loving Shepherd who still prepares a table before us, even in the presence of our enemies.

A VERY BRIEF WORD ON THEODICY

Many will ask the theodicy question: Why? And at some point in the future, spiritual leaders feeling their way through the valley of the shadow may be able to provide a tentative guess as an answer. Most often, the wisdom and purpose that arise out of human-caused disaster is retrospective. It may, in time, be clear that "all things work together for good," as Paul states in Romans 8:28, but such understandings generally emerge when the faith community is able to look backward, not in the moment. And those understandings that emerge after time are often richer and more profound than those offered in the urgent desperation of the moment. In the immediate aftermath of a human-caused disaster, set the theodicy question aside. Ask why? Plead why? Scream WHY?—but don't look too hard for an answer. People will ask. But the most compassionate and honest response to provide is simply: I don't know.

1

Phase One: Devastation and Heroism

A pastor in a community in the Midwest was having dinner with his family when his son called and said, "Turn on the television, something's happening at City Hall." What was happening was a mass shooting that took the lives of several citizens and gravely injured many, including the mayor. Though he did not know it at the time, some of those killed or injured were members of his congregation. The pastor left the restaurant and went over to City Hall, which was quite near the church. Panicked people were milling around. The EMTs, police, and other first respond-ers were doing their thing. The press with their cameras were shining bright lights into the darkness, speaking excitedly into microphones.

The pastor walked over to the welcome center of his church, and found the entire staff gathered around a small television, watching what the reporters were saying right outside their doors. He later said that as he looked around at his staff and the familiar surroundings in that terrible, strange moment, an inner voice addressed him: "This changes everything." He said to his colleagues, "Let's meet in the morning and begin to figure this out."

When a violent event shatters the normal life of a community, the "voice" that addresses us is the event itself, changing everything, chal-lenging us to stop, to notice everything, to pay attention, to be in the moment. What just happened? What do we do now? Violence and trauma can devastate a congregation. In the first hours and days, regardless of training and experience, people feel powerlessness, shock, denial, or disbelief. Whatever was scheduled in the life of the commu-nity shockingly is no longer the business for the day (or the many days ahead). In the chart on page xiv, this shock is signified by a discon-nected, sudden drop from "normal" to the onset of the disaster cycle that began with the incident. After a traumatic event, the primary goal for the pastoral leaders and congregation is the stabilization of the min-istry in that place.

Usually, an insistent internal pressure to act and respond in a help-ful way emerges in the immediate aftermath of violence. These valiant attempts to *fix* what has shattered—prayer chains, casserole assembly lines, child-care routines and carpools, grocery runs, vigils, memorials, worship planning, and an endless array of crafted gifts, cards, donations, and well-wishes—consume the first hours and days of response. The label for the common external reaction to the devastation is "Heroism." Heroism can have a positive quality. In those first hours and days, many logistics must be accomplished to get out of harm's way, gather people, communicate and inform, feed and shelter those in need, provide for worship, and express the presence of divine love in a tangible way. As people of faith, these heroic acts are part of who we are and what we do.

Heroism also has a negative quality. As long as we are *acting* we do not have to *feel*. Heroism can serve to distract us from the immeasurable pain of loss, which means it can also distract us from healing. As much as heroic acts are a part of who we are and what we do as a faithful people, slowing down and walking through the valley of the shadow of death with one another also shapes our significant character as children of God. Faith communities are natural places for people to gather to safely express devastation, to feel the pain of loss, and to talk about what has happened with others.

PASTORAL LEADERSHIP

"How the leader leads will influence how the community follows." A violent incident disrupts normal life. The phone rings and a distraught mother's voice stammers that her daughter, one of the girls in the youth group, is at the hospital because she was sexually assaulted at the local county fair. Or, there is breaking news streaming across the TV of a hostage incident occurring at your church, resulting in a double murder and suicide in the sanctuary. The news is devastating, and you feel a sense of shock, disbelief, and deep pain. It is common to feel a complete sense of incomprehension and paralysis. You may not know what to say or do. Traumatic events often overwhelm our usual ability to cope and respond. Ordination to ministry does not shield one from the effects of a traumatic incident. The impact experienced after trauma cannot be generalized or discounted. A traumatic event is shattering. It destabilizes one's sense of balance. It scrambles the brain. Trauma cannot be intellectualized away, no matter how much one may wish to do so. Dismissing the impact the event has on you will not be helpful to you or to those who need you. As counterintuitive as it may feel, best practices have shown that moving *through* this devastation phase is more helpful than trying to avoid it.

The first phase of response after violence is devastation, partly because there is no preparation. It blindsides everyone, and yet, leaders of a beloved faith community, whatever they may be feeling personally, are forced to deal with the impact of the event and shepherd the people through chaos.

Congregations that eventually thrive beyond a trauma incident have pastors who respond to what is now in their path. A leader who can be present immediately is extremely helpful: one who is willing to enter and stand with others in the most difficult of situations where shock and disbelief are raw and the pain is disturbing.

The art of pastoring in post-trauma situations is to be present to the volatility of the circumstances and the people in them while not over-functioning. It is vital to neither overreact nor rush heedlessly into the pain and devastation without emotional and spiritual preparation. Intuitively, a leader will want to just get in the car and go, but this is not very helpful. First, find a place where the tears can well up in your own eyes, where you can express your own hurt and be impacted by what has happened. Then breathe. Breathe for however long it takes. Find that place where the sense of inadequacy and uncertainty can be revealed—then breathe some more. Breathe and listen for the comforting words from within. As you listen, those words will come. Breathe, listen, breathe, and trust when choosing to enter the pain of devastation. Though it may not seem so, it is a kind of holy ground. Truthfully, ten, fifteen, or twenty minutes will not change the outcome of a situation; but those minutes of breathing and listening will change how you enter the event. A spiritual leader is a representative of something vast and mysterious. That leader needs to be completely present because, when the cameras begin clicking or when the piercing cries of a father are heard throughout hospital corridors, the pastor will be expected to respond. How one walks into that moment will make a difference and influence others. Pastoral leaders have an important shepherding role. Pastors are in the position to offer the best leadership and guidance under these conditions. Their influence greatly determines whether the people most impacted have the space and safety to be honest. Answers are not needed. What is needed most is an honest and caring presence.

The etymology of the word *devastation* suggests an emptying. Trauma takes life and takes the life out of survivors and those who lead them. It empties you. Spiritual leaders stand in that moment of devastation, offering a sense of stability and providing assurance. That's an important realization. Be intentional about entering the devastation as an assuring presence.

EMOTIONAL AND SPIRITUAL CARE NEEDS
FOLLOWING TRAUMA

On the first Sunday of Advent in a small town in the Northeast, the congregation and choir were singing the opening hymn, "My Lord, What a Morning!" The pastor was singing from the pulpit when she noticed out of the corner of her eye the door behind the choir loft opening. As she was wondering who was late to worship, an armed man stepped through the door and opened fire on his former wife, the church organist. As she fell to the floor and choir members rushed to help her, the man strode down the center aisle and out the sanctuary doors. Several minutes later, he returned "to finish the task," and though church members blocked the door, they yielded when he threatened to shoot them. He returned to the organ, fired again into the prone body of the organist, and was then tackled, disarmed, and subdued by the pastor and members of the choir. Though it seemed like hours, the pastor said later, it was only ten minutes before emergency responders and police arrived and took the man into custody. The thirty or so congregants were separated and interviewed for hours following the service. The organist, a longtime church member and friend of the pastor, was pronounced dead at the scene.

A couple of days later, the entire congregation was invited to participate in a conversation and share a fellowship meal with the pastor and a professional disaster responder. During that event, church members, ranging in age from fourteen to eighty-four, wept and struggled to re-create, remember, and make sense of what had happened to them. Again and again they compared memories, corrected each other, then lapsed into confused silence when the time and event sequences didn't—couldn't add up to a coherent narrative. Several spoke with naked anguish of their sense of shame and guilt that they hadn't been able to stop the shooter from re-entering the sanctuary and killing their friend. Others cringed visibly while the story was retold.

Two members of the congregation who were present that Sunday had said they would be there that night, but did not show up: one forgot, another accepted an out-of-town assignment. Several reported sleeplessness and nightmares. A memorial of candles had been established on the steps of the sanctuary; several members went by daily to sit and look at the light, or to tend the memorial and make sure it remained intact. Some weeks later, the pastor reported that a couple of members had quit attending after becoming angry about issues unrelated to the shooting. The congregation did not return to their sanctuary until after Epiphany, six weeks later. Although they held a ritual cleansing and rededication of the sanctuary, many members continued to feel uncomfortable there.

Common reactions to trauma may include: fear, anxiety, numbness, sadness, depression, anger and rage, negativity, moodiness, impatience or irritability, changes in appetite, nightmares or flashbacks, increased use of alcohol/drugs, avoidance, difficulty in sleeping, and loss of interest in previous activities. For most people, these effects dissipate in time, without outside intervention. Extreme or extended expression of these reactions in an individual may signify that that person is not naturally healing from the impact of the event and may need additional attention or therapeutic intervention.

Therapists who treat trauma identify three things that support healing and recovery for those who have experienced or witnessed a traumatic event: connection or relationship, narrative (a way to tell their story), and relaxation. For most people and communities, this means finding ways (verbal and symbolic) to tell the story and unpack the impact of the event in the presence of a trusted friend or spiritual guide; beginning to integrate the event with others in community; and embracing moments of relaxation and grace.

Faith communities, by nature, are uniquely well equipped to support these basic, life-giving practices, especially in the wake of a violent event. The rituals of worship provide a reliable and familiar path through the valley of the shadow. The community's sacred text and salvation story offer the "bones" of a transformative narrative to be adapted and adopted as survivors and witnesses begin to tell their own stories. A congregation's fellowship practices and sustaining belief in the importance of connection between and among people as a channel of divine presence and blessing are avenues for the deepening of connectedness. They extend an invitation to reach out for support and relationship that will not require extraordinary effort for persons whose spiritual and emotional resources have been strained by the impact of the event on their lives. People who live alone or who lack strong primary relationships, as well as those with families and friends, can find solace, support, and a place to tell their story when the faith community gathers in the wake of violence.

STAFF AND LAY EXPERIENCES

After violence or trauma, members of the *church staff* need attention and assurance as well. Attentiveness, assessment, and assurance are constant themes in trauma response. Staff members have a vital role to play throughout the recovery and healing process. In the immediate aftermath, they answer the phones, run interference, disburse information, provide comfort and care, support youth group members, shepherd the Sunday school teachers, control access, deal with insurance companies, and clean up the mess. They have deep relationships with members and are leaders in the core ministries of the congregation. They are important in helping to stabilize the ministry of a traumatized congregation.

Depending on the size of a congregation, staff may include a youth director, musicians, school staff, administrative and building/maintenance personnel. Each one needs someone to stand with them as they experience the impact of the incident. Staff members are not immune, and even if they appear to be "handling things well" and getting their work done, they are affected physically, emotionally, and spiritually. They may be experiencing social or even financial consequences as a result of trauma, which complicate their response to this incident. Trauma disrupts the survivor's normal state of balance, wellness, and safety. Like the pastoral leaders, staff members are trying to cope. They have their "normal" job responsibilities and are expected to shoulder these along with the extraordinary stuff that violence and trauma brings.

A pastor has the responsibility to tend to the church staff, to be attentive, and to remember that each one has a life outside the office, a life that may become more vulnerable in the wake of trauma. As staff members are well supported by leaders, they will be better equipped, in turn, to care for the congregation and community. Help them be attentive to the most critical next steps, staying focused on what is more pressing. Designing the poster for next month's all-church picnic can be delayed! Provide leadership and compassion. Be present and honest, and communicate clearly. This will help alleviate problems and decrease anxiety.

Lay leaders will also need and expect attentiveness. For the pastor, there is no dimension where leadership energy will not be required. The pastoral leader has a daunting task and will be seen as the head by those in the congregation and beyond it—regardless of whether he or she feels adequate to the task. Among these important congregational leaders, some may be directly affected, others indirectly, and a few may seem not bothered at all. Because of these varying degrees of distress, it is important not to generalize in planning and providing pastoral care. Don't spend a lot of energy assessing who falls into what category. Trust yourself and the Spirit's working in you and them. Their impact will be revealed through the course of moving forward in ways that encourage honest expression and constructive care.

As noted above, successful therapeutic interventions typically share three common characteristics: the expression of narrative (telling the story), the experience of trusted connection or relationship, and relaxation, or self-regulation. Among people of faith, these same characteristics apply. First, staff and lay leaders need opportunities to express what happened—how they were affected or not. Second, they need connection, to get together. They need to be offered opportunities to tell their story or express their distress in a safe environment and to be reassured that trauma-related symptoms are normal reactions to the event. Pastors and others who listen to and support these persons need to do so in a relaxed body; further, they need to model a calm presence that can be mirrored by those who are talking about what has happened and what is happening to them. If someone does not have words, create opportunities for nonverbal expressions as well.

Accurate communication is essential. Staff, along with people in the congregation (especially lay leaders), need to know what's going on. A quick daily email, a brief post, or short voice messages on the church phone can serve as instruments to keep leaders informed. What, who, and where—direct and accurate information is all that's needed. Do not write a treatise or sermonize. The leaders want to know basic information about what their pastor and church are doing and how they can be helpful and supportive. Creating strong communication channels will be helpful during the long journey of healing.

CONGREGATIONAL CARE

After the police finished debriefing everyone who had been present in worship the day of the shooting, worried family members and friends gathered their loved ones up and took them home for comfort and care. The next day was a work day, after all, and many felt the best thing was just to get back into a normal routine as soon as possible. The building in which the sanctuary was located remained closed, sealed off with crime scene tape; the message on the answering machine directed people to the nearby church house and said worship would be held, until further notice, in the Fellowship Hall there.

The pastor, staff, elders, and deacons came together at a breakfast meeting early Monday, trying to process their own shock and grief while beginning to develop a plan to care for the congregation. The pastor reported that her colleagues from the town's nearby churches had decided to hold candlelight prayer services each night that week, so that the community could gather to grieve. Grief counselors would be present, light snacks would be served following, and everyone hoped their neighbors from First United would be a part of the services, without feeling that they had to do anything.

The church administrator came out of the office and placed a stack of call sheets on the table. Thirty of the church's two hundred members had left messages overnight, ranging from offers to help in whatever way they could to questions about the shooter and the status of the sanctuary. What meetings would be held? Cancelled? What about worship? Choir practice? Seven of the calls were from members whose voices clearly indicated they were profoundly affected by what had happened: they wept audibly, raged at the lack of security that allowed the shooter easy access to the church, or spoke in a monotone so unlike their normal tone that it seemed evident they were numb with shock. The pastor and chair of the board of deacons, a psychotherapist, looked at each other and took a deep breath. "The church is Christ, embodied as community. How can we be the presence of Christ here and now?" the pastor said, and everyone, for just a second, felt a fluttering possibility of peace. It was the trademark phrase she always used before every meeting, in every prayer: in this hard moment, hearing it again felt to all of them like a benediction.

"Yea, though I walk through the valley of the shadow of death, you are with me." Congregational care in the aftermath of a public violence event is a many-layered, subtle work. We have become "alien[s] residing in a foreign land" (Exod. 2:22), yearning for a glimpse of the presence of God, for a healing word, for the touch of another's hand, so that we might know that we have not been left alone in the chaos. Yet this "foreign land" of trauma's aftermath is also, deeply, a place where we take off our shoes and know we walk on holy ground. In the story from Exodus, Moses was a shepherd, tending his father-in-law's flock in the wilderness of Midian, when one day he noticed a bush burning in the desert. Leaving his flock, Moses turned aside to see the bush, which kept on burning but was not consumed. He heard a voice: "Moses! . . . Remove the sandals from your feet, for the place on which you are standing is holy ground" (Exod. 3:3–5). An act of public violence is a kind of burning bush: something so out of our normal experiencing that it draws us away from our ordinary responsibilities, catches us up short, and causes us to stop in our tracks. And we should.

Jewish *midrash* (interpretative stories) offer an alternative reading of that moment that changed Moses' life, and the life of his people, forever. It suggests that another way to read or translate the words "Remove your sandals" is "change your habits, turn a different way." On the holy ground of congregational life following an event of violence, when it seems that the shock, pain, and anger are a fire that will burn unceasingly, this reading of Exodus offers powerful advice to pastors and church leaders: *Change your habits, turn a different way.* After a traumatic event, life will not look like it did before, nor should it. On the holy ground of a community's wounding, we are invited, first to stop and be attentive, and next to turn a different way. In the short term, we will see all congregational practice through the lens of compassionate care and spiritual meaning-making.

CHILDREN, YOUTH, AND CAREGIVERS

Talking to children about actual violence comes down to a few core elements: being a reliable, trustworthy adult, telling the truth, letting children or youth guide the conversation, and encouraging safety.

Be a reliable, trustworthy adult for children and youth around you. Children need trustworthy adults in their lives in order to grow and develop well. Reliability establishes a sense of safety for both children and adolescents.

Tell the truth. When discussing a tragedy, stick to basic facts of the case. Do not embellish, and do not use euphemisms or metaphors. Be specific and simple.

Let the children and youth guide the conversation. A child's age and developmental level will influence what questions they ask and how they respond to adults sharing with them. Some children will be ready to talk about meaningful topics sooner than expected, while others will not be interested or may not have developed capacities to handle challenging topics. Create the safe space for them to process at their own pace by following their lead, curiosity, and insistence.

Preschoolers tend to be very concrete.

Elementary school kids often express more empathy and make more connections than younger children. Not wanting to talk is common too. Do not force them to talk. Simply let them know that, if they have questions or concerns at any time, you are available for conversation.

Teenagers will express a wide range of responses. Like children, some may not have words, and will prefer to be quiet or be reminded of safety and routine around home, school, or church. All will need their own spaces apart from family and their congregation as well as with their family and congregation to move through the aftermath of trauma. Like all forms of pastoral and congregational leadership, youth ministry in the aftermath of violence requires good self-care of the leaders, compassionate presence, and artful discernment for what appears most helpful to this group of youth.

Encourage safety. Include children and youth in creating responses to tragedy by incorporating their spontaneous gestures and interest into ordinary experiences, as they arise, and also through intentional community memorializing. Stories can be shared by talking but also without words. You may pray together, listen to music, draw or paint, play games, or exercise together. You may sing or play instruments together, or incorporate special foods or candle lighting into your snack or mealtimes.

Whatever you do, do not try to pretend away or ignore the truth while you are with the children of your congregation and among your families. Avoiding the truth, especially when children are in close proximity to a tragic event, produces deleterious effects on family and social systems and on children's senses of well-being.

Being in these relationships with children is not about having answers. It is about practicing whole self living within the frameworks of faith, hope, and love.

THE PRESS AND THE PROBLEM VOLUNTEER

After any public violence event, local and sometimes even national press become a powerful and visible presence in a community; trying to report on the event, get the story, and find people, pictures, and insights that will illuminate the story as it unfolds. In our experience, many reporters and film crews are deeply affected by what they are seeing and reporting, care about the story they are telling, and see their work as a way to help support awareness in the larger community and the healing of those affected. The press are not the enemy; they are partners in the unfolding story of a violent event and its aftermath, and the impact on persons and communities. Spiritual leaders, themselves affected by a tragedy, sometimes make the mistake of viewing the press as an opposing force, rather than enlisting them in helping the congregation to weave and share the faith story it is beginning to live out in the aftermath of the event. Rather than barring access to the congregation and its services, meet with representatives of the media and offer to provide structured access so that they can help others see faith in the midst of crisis.

Many churches that have had such experiences suggest a few simple guidelines that helped them create a positive relationship between the media and the community of faith.

1. *Don't shut them out.* If the church doesn't share its story, the media will find another story to tell. This is a faith story that is unfolding, a rare opportunity to show how people of faith care for one another, reach out for divine comfort, lament their losses with honesty, and make meaning in the wake of a senseless tragedy. In the Christian tradition, and in the wake of public violence, "evangelism" is sharing the news of a saving story with those in the larger community who may lack such a story. There are many people who will watch this story unfold, hoping to find connection, meaning, and hope. The media is an important part of the way a connection can be made with people in the larger community who may be struggling, isolated, or seeking hope.

2. *Appoint one primary contact.* The pastor is a natural choice, unless the impact of the event involved him or her directly. The pastor is the lead storyteller in the congregation: in this circumstance, more than ever, her voice or his shaping of the story is central to how the community will hear and process what has happened.

Additionally, choose one or two people in the congregation or staff to be the primary points of access for questions and interviews with the press.

3. *Limit the disruption.* If there are multiple media outlets present following the event, choose one primary reporter and film crew to record services of worship or funerals, and set up a feed line so that others can have access. Instruct that team to work from an unobtrusive place, perhaps in the rear of the sanctuary or from the balcony, and not to move about and create a distraction in the service.

4. *Preserve peoples' privacy and dignity.* Instruct the film crew not to film people's faces or to approach anyone while in the sanctuary. If individuals wish to be interviewed outside the sanctuary following a service, they may do so, respecting the limits and the wishes of everyone.

The publicity that attends an act of public violence often attracts what are sometimes referred to as "SUVs": spontaneous uninvited volunteers. They will hear of the event, and believe that they have a calling, a unique responsibility, or a special message to deliver to survivors and the traumatized community. They may be religious extremists, persons with emotional or mental illness, or well-intended but unaware people who feel moved by what has happened and want to be a part of the work of recovery. Some of these people may be more difficult than others. If you can politely thank them and turn them away from their intention of involvement, do so. If they are less amenable to a respectful approach, it is appropriate to have them removed from the premises. In some extreme cases, it may even be necessary to have local law enforcement restrain or remove such persons.

Some congregations have found it helpful to have a local law enforcement professional and/or a mental health clinician present at public congregational gatherings following an event, to keep an eye out for SUVs and manage them as necessary. After the shooting in Tucson, Arizona, in January 2011 that wounded Congresswoman Gabrielle Giffords and killed several others, a team of national responders was asked to provide this service at the funeral for Christina-Taylor Green, the young girl and "September 11 baby" who was killed by the gunman. There were thousands of persons present outside the sanctuary, a report that members of a hate group from the Westboro Baptist Church were going to demonstrate, and widespread anxiety that there could be disruptions that would distract the family and church from their worship and grieving. Along with some community chaplains and pastors, responders moved among the various groups gathered in witness and solidarity, keeping an eye out for any potential problem. Also in Tucson, at another church, one of the responders was able to intercept a well-intentioned but inappropriate neighboring minister from intruding on the service for another of those killed, encouraging him to leave the property and return home.

COMMUNITY-WIDE CARE

In the immediate aftermath of a human-caused disaster, there is a tremendous outpouring of emotions— shock, grief, dismay, anger, hatred, compassion, frustration, disbelief, the need to shelter as well as the need to be together—as people struggle to make sense of the senseless. As the pastor and congregation engage with the wider community following public violence, these expressions of solidarity are typically a part of public life in the immediate aftermath of an event: the community-wide candlelight prayer vigil; a community-wide secular event; and an outpouring of compassion that, unless channeled appropriately, may inundate your community in ways that are not helpful.

Community-Wide Candlelight Prayer Vigil

In almost every instance of public violence, a community-wide candle-light prayer vigil gathers neighbors who need to express their sorrow as one. In the face of unimaginable horror and loss, the community longs to gather together, often near the scene of the event or the location of an impromptu memorial. Here are some considerations regarding the community-wide candlelight prayer vigil.

Should an affected pastor plan or be involved in the service? The answer to this is a qualified yes. Based on the type of event and the proximity of the congregation to the trauma, a pastor or faith leader may be too overwhelmed with providing care to others to plan the event, but will want to participate. The pastor should be visible with the faith community, giving witness to the presence of God in the midst of chaos.

Pastoral leaders in close proximity to the trauma bring unique per-spective to bear on the content of the vigil or the message generated. One of the things to be aware of is the proximity question. For pastors who have had congregational members killed during a human-caused disaster, while other clergy in the community did not, the theological message and means of expression may be very different from other col-leagues in the larger community.

I remember in the immediate aftermath of a shooting, an email from the moderator of our local ministerial alliance announced we would gather in the town square later that evening. One of the clergy without congre-gants affected by the event "took the lead" in organizing the prayer vigil. She proposed a theme of "hope and healing." After spending the night before in the ER with the spouse of one of those killed, waiting for him to show up and realizing he wasn't coming, which was confirmed with the arrival of the police chaplain, I had no energy to get involved in the planning of the event. I felt pretty sure this was a time for the body of Christ to do its thing, and I allowed others to plan. But when the email

announcing "hope and healing" as the focus of the first candlelight vigil
on the night after a massacre was circulated, I realized I needed to speak
into the situation. I wrote a very ungracious "reply all" and asked that
we focus on lament and brokenness and mystery and hurting and simply
being together. Thankfully, the leader of the event took my encourage-
ment to heart and reworked the event around the idea of "standing
together."

Be involved in the candlelight vigil. Be authentic in whatever part
you have. Insofar as possible, model appropriate emotions. This is not
the time to be brave and carry on and overcome. This is a time to stand
in the valley of the shadow of death (and dismay and disbelief and
distress) and acknowledge hurt, woundedness, and the painful inability
to make sense of the senselessness of violence and trauma. The time
for hope and healing will come, just not at the first community-wide
candlelight vigil.

Community-Wide Secular Events

Typically, a community-wide candlelight vigil occurs on the first or second night after an event. For some events with a big emotional impact
upon the community, another, more secular event can be helpful. In
the case of an event with multiple deaths, the affected community will
spend days, even weeks attending funerals and vigils and other worship
services. The horror of the event will be replayed nonstop on the news
and will be relived with each additional service. If the death of a child
was involved, the emotional trauma will be even greater.

Sometimes, for the good of the community, a community-wide
secular event is needed to provide a safe and appropriate outlet for all
emotions and as a way for people to affirm (again) the goodness of life.
The focus of this event will emerge from the context of the situation.
In Tucson, after the January 2011 mass shooting, the leaders of the
ecumenical faith community gathered to figure out what to do. During
that meeting, the idea to have a children's day on the campus of the
local university emerged. Due to the death of a young girl, nine-year-
old Christina-Taylor Green, the focus was on children and activities
that could bring families together.

Pastoral leaders may be in a position to assist in the creation of
a community-wide secular event, if they or their congregation are
not overly impacted by the immediacy of the violent or trauma. Be

attentive to the needs of the community and the direction of the conversations being held. Sometimes there is a tremendous up-swell in "do-gooding" that initiates a frenzy of communal activities, engaged without much thought as to their usefulness or how they will conclude. Be wary of getting caught up in the frenzy. Be intentional about time and resources before committing to be a part of the new "overcoming differences" committee (or whatever gets created in the community by those who want to "do good for others"). New initiatives and groups may spring into action in the immediate aftermath of a violent event. In many cases, these groups provide a way to vent emotional energy and, as such, are useful in the moment for those who need to be doing, even though the groups may have little, if any, long-term impact on the community. So be intentional about involvement in anything that is longer than a one-time event.

CHANNELING THE OUTPOURING OF COMPASSION

One of the most useful things to do in the immediate aftermath of an event is to create a way to channel the outpouring of compassion that may flood a congregation and community, and to prepare for all the stuff—teddy bears, cards, clothes, bracelets, books, pies, barbeque—that may show up, inundate, and overwhelm congregations and communities.

In response to the shooting at Sandy Hook Elementary School in Newtown, Connecticut, nearly 80,000 teddy bears in total were delivered to schools, firehouses, police stations, houses of worship, and many other locations within the community of about 30,000 people. There were so many bears (and other items sent from around the world) that special receiving and storage facilities were needed immediately. People want to reach out and offer hope in the aftermath of terrible tragedies. Unfortunately, they don't often think through the effect their "act of compassion" has upon a devastated community. Just as a community affected by a tornado doesn't need a semi-trailer full of mattresses delivered—no matter how well intentioned (as there are no houses to put the mattresses into)—communities affected by human-caused disasters are often equally ill-equipped to accept the "gifts" that are sent their way by those who care.

One easy way to help channel compassion in the aftermath of a human-caused disaster is to publicize the opportunity to designate gifts to vetted and trustworthy local or national disaster-response agencies. Congregations may already have a practice of giving to their denomination's disaster-response agency or other well-known groups. If not, a fund can be specifically created to support the long-term recovery through one of those agencies or a trusted local group. Then publicize the existence of the fund in the media and online through social media. This way people can offer gifts of compassion (checks) that can be used to support the disaster response; and well-meant expressions of compassion do not create another, unanticipated burden on people already overwhelmed by violence and trauma.

LAST BUT NOT LEAST: CLERGY SELF-CARE

In the aftermath of trauma, self-care will be essential to strengthen capacity for leadership in this season. Self-care is a vital element of professional well-being, even prior to a violent incident. Regular exercise, checking in with a therapist, participating in a peer group, having a spiritual director, meeting with a nutritionist, attending regular checkups at the doctor's office, creating intentional time away for prayer and contemplation, being actively engaged in civic groups, enjoying hobbies—all these are elements of a good self-care plan. In the immediate aftermath of violence, regular routines are often decimated as the immediate needs of the people involved overwhelm the rhythms of everyday life. Yet self-care in the days and weeks following a traumatic event is critical. As the adage goes, "Put on your own oxygen mask first before helping others." Self-care is about tending *you*. It may seem selfish or something that can be done "later" but sustaining good leadership dictates that self-care is the most important task in the aftermath of a human-caused disaster.

A few principles for congregational leaders following trauma:

— *Offer yourself (and others) grace.* Everyone responds to violence and trauma differently. Your response, no matter what it is, is normal and acceptable. Be gracious to yourself and those in your congregation. What seems odd or inappropriate on an ordinary day may be normal in the immediate aftermath of a disaster.

— *Beware of frenzy.* Realize the adrenaline is pumping and the desire to help may be in hyperdrive. Be careful about trying to be available for all who are suffering. One can quickly become overwhelmed in trying to provide care in the context of pain and chaos while still attempting to perform daily duties. Realize you are only one person, and you have a job to do—to lead the people of God. Your job is *not* to care for everyone. Your job is to provide appropriate care and, as able, empower others to do the same.

—*Focus on the basics.* Worship matters. A meeting of the congregation matters. At times of great distress, the community of faith wants to see and hear from the pastor; often, the first time that occurs is the first worship service after an event. Focus on that worship experience: pick different hymns, appropriate readings, and send your pre-trauma planned sermon through the shredder.

—*Make space.* As soon as possible and appropriate, get out of the affected community or context. Drive out of town, or two towns over, and have lunch where people are not devastated by what happened. Realize that "normal" life is still happening around you and your congregation. Even though it will feel odd and frustrating at some level, getting out of the context of the human-caused disaster will provide needed perspective on what needs to be done.

—*Review the calendar.* In the week after a human-caused disaster, get out your calendar and cancel all non-essential events, meetings, and commitments. And be honest about what is "non-essential." The judicatory meeting you are chairing is non-essential. Your trip to the stewardship conference is non-essential. Make space in your calendar for time to sit, pray, read, relax, eat dinner with a spouse or friend, or take a slow walk by a lake. This is also true for congregational events (Bible study, luncheons, fellowship events, concerts); cancel them in the week (or weeks) following a human-caused disaster, or reframe them to provide support and care for those in the community affected by the event. By doing this you are modeling a healthy and appropriate response for others: "This is a big deal, and we need to attend to its impact on us as individuals and as a group." This is *not* the time to join the newly forming "understanding violence" group that the church down the road may be offering to the community. There will be time to get more involved in the community's process of discernment and reflection about the event. Now is not that time.

—*Preach.* Be in the pulpit the next couple (three or four) of Sundays. If the associate pastor or someone else is scheduled to preach, change it. As the pastor of the congregation, you need to be in the pulpit in the weeks following a traumatic event. Vocational trauma often results from a human-caused disaster. One's call, one's sense of personal mission, professional dreams, and the course imagined for the congregation you lead are all impacted by a violent event. Being in the pulpit is not just good for the congregation; it is good for you and for the work you will do in the months that follow, in reconstructing your sense of call.

—*Be authentic.* There is often a private/public split in how spiritual leaders respond to a violent event that affects the congregations they serve. People tend to be privately devastated and publicly optimistic. Too often, leaders proclaim publicly: "We will not let this event change us!" But when a member of the youth group was killed by a drunk driver, a colleague committed suicide, an arson fire ripped through and destroyed fellowship hall, a shooter opened fire; all these events are shattering, and *should* change, challenge, and in time, perhaps enrich faith and the experience of the divine presence. Allow grief, anger, disgust, lament, frustration, and unknowing to come forth in intentional ways during worship and in the course of everyday life in interaction with others who are wondering, "Is it okay to cry, or do I have to pretend this event never happened?" It's okay to walk into a staff meeting, a congregant's house, or the pulpit on Sunday and share that your heart too is broken.

—*Be with supportive people.* Make space to have dinner and drinks with family and friends, people it is okay to simply "be with" and not have to "care for" in any professional capacity. It's okay to be reminded that life carries on, even with a broken heart, and that the concerns of one's spouse, children, and friends continue to be valid.

RESILIENCE: A HOPEFUL NOTE

The vast majority of people possess the emotional and spiritual resources to recover from trauma without intervention, and will benefit from and contribute to healing practices rooted in the life of the congregation, worship, and fellowship. A small percentage of persons do not recover naturally from trauma. They may be persons with cumulative or prior exposure to traumatic events, or post-traumatic stress, whose coping skills are diminished; individuals in crisis for other reasons, or who live with mental illness. They may have none of these known circumstances but be acting atypically in a way that is ongoing and arouses concern. For these few individuals, pastoral caregivers will want to seek referral to professional support or treatment, and should have trusted clinicians to recommend to their church members who may require such attention.

For the rest of us, practices embedded in the DNA of faith are integral to the work of healing and will be potent forces supporting the resilient rebounding of a congregation and community. The task is to remain generous, grateful, open, and patient as pastors and congregations begin to feel their way through the strange land of loss and lament. St. Francis of Assisi was quoted as having said: "Preach the gospel in all seasons. If necessary, use words." The visibility of a community of faith and its neighbors working together to lament, help, and heal one another in the wake of public violence is a sacred story: a potent, visible witness to the deep truth and meaning we find when living out faith in the valley of the shadow. Worship is the community of faith's central expression of this story and witness. The next chapter addresses how worship and liturgy may be reimagined in the wake of trauma to support the broken heart of the people of God.

2

Worship and Theology after Trauma

On the quiet campus of the state university, five students were killed outright and several more wounded in the lecture hall before the man who shot them turned the gun on himself and died. It was Thursday afternoon, and since the campus was put on immediate lockdown, most of the pastors whose churches were near campus convened in the city's one hospital, to support the families and faculty who were gathered waiting for news. All but one of the hospitalized students eventually recovered and most were released by the weekend. The associate pastor of one of the churches was to lead worship that Sunday. Nothing she had learned in seminary had prepared her for this Sunday, but she knew it was possibly the most important service she would ever lead.

In the endless hours and bewildering days following trauma, worship holds the broken heart of the people. Ritual gives shape to the chaos of grief, anger, and disbelief, weaving a journey through the valley of the shadow. The green pastures and still waters that restore the soul are far off in a distance that can be scarcely glimpsed through tears. Worship in the valley of the shadow is a liminal space, a spiritual threshold. It holds impossible questions, ancient affirmations, and inchoate yearnings in equal value, regardless of their apparent contradiction, so that the people of God can begin to sing the Lord's song in the strange land of the aftermath of violence. What the worship leaders choose to do in the moment, and how the congregation is invited into this hard and holy space, is of critical importance and will shape the narrative of lament and healing for the whole community.

People of faith, and even people whose spirituality is non-religious, need to gather as soon as possible following a violent event. To be together—to sit with others in silence, to weep, to pray, to keep vigil with candles and songs and sacred words—provides grounding when the impossible has happened. It establishes a safety net within which shocked and grieving survivors and witnesses may begin to express anger and sorrow, hurt and hope. Many communities of faith in proximity to a public violence event find that throwing open their doors immediately for the community to gather together— even when they do not have time to write a formal service—is an act of hospitality and grace. Make liturgical space available to grieve and pray together. Reach across the customary boundaries of faiths or denominations and *be together*. There is healing power in the gathering of the whole community, no matter the particular faith of its members.

In the first weeks following a violent event in a community, worship should provide an environment of spiritual safety and openness. Members will need comfort and want to experience connection with God and with others. Worship offers a space to articulate the complex feelings evoked by trauma. The congregation's "ordinary time" story has been disrupted by a violent event; for the short term, this event has, in a profound way, shattered their salvation story. Who God is, how God saves (or doesn't), what this means to the way people understand life and faith, are all called into question. This is normal, and even, in a way, desirable. The Christian narrative itself was profoundly shaped by violence, as were those of its Jewish and Muslim siblings, and the shape of those narratives can support faith communities as they struggle to voice their own journeys through chaos.

The narrative of the exodus was born in violence and continued through a long wilderness wandering. The people suffered hunger and fear. They experienced and voiced a sense of abandonment by the divine presence. In the Christian Gospels, Jesus' followers gathered in fellowship one night, only to scatter the next day, terrified, as they witnessed the violent torture and death of their teacher and friend. After Jesus' murder, disciples felt abandoned by God. They fought among themselves and despaired.

Most communities of faith lean on these constitutive narratives with a casual familiarity that belies their power. In times of chaos, those holy stories become true and real in ways never imagined. The task of the worship leader and pastor is to allow Scripture and ritual practice to support a congregation as it begins to tell a new and painful story, and to locate that story in the sacred narratives of their faith. Find examples of "first Sunday" orders of worship (traditional and contemporary), bulletins for community vigil services and anniversary marker services in appendixes 3 and 5. Ideas for each part of the service described below are found in appendixes 4 and 6.

PLANNING THE FIRST SERVICE: WORSHIP REIMAGINED

Think of an ordinary traditional service as organized in three or four movements—Gathering, Listening, Sharing the Eucharist, Responding and Sending. Set aside for the moment the movement of Eucharist, which not all traditions observe weekly, and reframe those movements on this first Sunday *after* the tragedy:

> *Letting Go* (we release what was and seek sanctuary in the presence of God)
> *Letting Be* (we are present to God and to one another in the midst of distress)
> *Letting Begin* (our walk and work in the valley of the shadow begins)

Letting Go: We Come Seeking Sanctuary

When people gather following a traumatic event, powerful negative feelings and a sense of painful disorientation are involved. Some will be wondering how God can be present at all after what has happened. The words spoken in the opening of this service recognize the holiness of these painful feelings and at the same time express the longing people feel for connection with God and with one another in this valley of shadows. Words of invitation that acknowledge what has happened *and* the continuing presence of God are simple, clear, and true ways to begin the service. They are the beginning of the work of lament.

The Call to Worship and Opening Sentences set the tone for the worshiping community. Consider the opening words carefully. For example, a traditional call to worship begins, "The Lord is in his holy temple, let all the earth keep silence before God." This doesn't begin to capture this moment, this Sunday, so different from any Sunday that has gone before. *Is* God in the holy temple? Does the temple even seem "holy," on this day in which sorrow and confusion fill the air, crowding out peace? What are we doing here, on this day?

The work of this moment is lament, so the call to worship, the first words on this first Sunday *after*, should set the liturgical tone for the beginning of a journey the faith community will take together into the valley of the shadow.

It is more helpful to lead with something like, "Yea, though I walk through the valley of the shadow of death, I will fear no evil, for you are with me." Yes, the community is in the dark valley, *and yet* still in the presence of God. There is room here for hurt and hunger, for despair and desire, for rage, grief, confusion and anxiety, as well as hope, to be a part of the words the church addresses to God, as the community prays and sings and strains to listen for a word *from* God in the midst of an empty silence that is difficult to bear.

Hymns of Adoration usually open Sunday worship, but today is a day of sorrow, anger, and confusion. Even God's praise needs to honor that reality.

Text matters. Words matter. Let the opening hymn create a climate of support and reassurance. Let it open the way into lament. Since a sense of familiarity helps people feel grounded, also take care to choose hymn tunes well known by the congregation. The first hymn might begin to voice the feelings of grief and anger that often rise in the aftermath of a violent trauma, as well as express longings for hope and healing. In general, this is *not* the time for hymns about forgiveness; it is far too soon for that. Further, be sensitive about language: hymns with graphic language about blood and dying may be too evocative of what has just happened, shutting people down instead of drawing them into sacred space. This is a moment to model that praise can coexist with pain, that negative emotions are valid expressions of faith.

Confession of Sin. In many traditions the first movement of worship includes a time for corporate and personal confession of sin. "If we say that we have no sin, we deceive ourselves, and the truth is not in us" are the words that call many congregations to confession each Sunday, but not today. There is a need for truth in confession, especially after trauma, as members grapple with what has happened and how it makes them feel. To say that survivors who have just witnessed unspeakable evil committed in an act of violence or terror are unworthy of grace or have failed in the eyes of God is unhelpful. Congregants after trauma already feel the weight of sin in the world. Evil has been graphically demonstrated in plain sight. They do not need a suggestion that their negative feelings of anger or abandonment by God are sinful. They do not need to be further burdened by a sense of futility and failure. Confession may be reimagined on this Sunday as an acknowledgment of human powerlessness and despair over the powers and principalities that wreak violence in the world.

For this service, instead of a confession of sin, consider a confession of brokenness. Today, what the church needs to "confess" is far more complicated than the traditional call to confession that declares we are sinners in need of redemption. It is important to confess that the world is a far darker place than we had ever imagined. There is power in admitting that all our efforts to see good and bring good into the world feel, in this moment, false and futile. It is okay to confess that people are scared, angry, empty, and fearful that God is not going to show up. Believers need to acknowledge that the world, and our faith, are upside down, and we don't know where to turn. Let the words of invitation to confession, and the confessional prayer itself, embrace this wider understanding and turn the congregation's face toward lament, a deeply honest confession of heartbreak when so much is wrong around and within us.

After a call to confession, before common prayer, it may be very helpful to leave space for silence, maybe even a little more silence than customary. Breathe into the silence an awareness that holds all that is in the room—all the feelings and fears—in holy hands. In a unison prayer of confession, understand that the very rhythm of the people speaking words in unison creates a heartbeat, a pattern that stabilizes and assures: we walk in the valley of the shadow, *and* we walk with God.

Assurance of Pardon. Even more than on ordinary days, the assurance of pardon provides words of reassurance for a people whose sense of well-being and trust in the goodness of life has been disrupted. In this affirmation, let the people know: "God is our refuge and strength" (Ps. 46:1). Let them believe that their feelings of brokenness and anger are appropriate expressions of faith in this moment. Tell them that those feelings are held by the Spirit of God, who "helps us in our weakness . . . [and] intercedes with sighs too deep for words" (Rom. 8:26). Pouring water into the baptismal font as a ritual act at the beginning of confession or during the words of reassurance can be a potent and comforting reminder of our belonging to one another and to God in baptism.

Sharing the Peace is a ritual used by some congregations, placed variously at the beginning or close of worship, or, as suggested here, as a concluding symbolic action of unity following the confession and assurance of pardon. It is the love of God that has made the people one: and this day, more than ever, members of the congregation need to know and feel they are not alone; they belong to each other and to God.

Children's Time. Some churches invite children to come forward and hear a brief message from the pastor or another trusted adult. Confirm that the person responsible on the first Sunday after trauma is comfortable leading, and understands clearly what kind of message will be most helpful. It may be important to the children and their parents to hear from their pastor on this particular day. Be simple, truthful, loving, and reassuring. Say that many grown-ups are very sad today, and tell them, in plain words, why. Let them know that they are safe, and loved, and that God loves and embraces them. They can come to a parent or trusted grown-up if they feel frightened or confused. Tell them concrete ways that they can take care of one another, and be like Jesus for one another, especially when people are sad or hurting.

Letting Be: We Listen for a Word from God

The next movement of worship invites the community into a mode of listening and receiving. The texts for this Sunday include Scripture, but also the more disturbing "word" imposed by violence and trauma, and the unsettling words, perhaps yet unspoken, of the disrupted faith of believers who have had their trust in the good order of God's creation challenged. It will be important to make room for all of these texts to be present and acknowledged in worship.

The Prayer of Illumination. The longing to hear a word from God is even more poignant today. The simple words of this prayer should support listeners, in the midst of confusion and the aftermath of violence, to quiet themselves and open their hearts to receive a word of grace.

First Reading. A psalm—especially a psalm of lament—can be a powerful reminder that the sacred texts of our ancestors in faith have already been where the church finds itself today: lost, confused, and bereft. Let the old words say what is difficult to express. Psalms 23, 46, 90, 91, or 121 are good choices. According to denominational or congregational practice, readings may be guided by the lectionary each Sunday.

The Sermon. If the sermon has been prepared already, *before* what happened, put it away for another time, or shred it. As the congregation begins its work of lament, the words of this message need to say, "Even though we walk through the valley of the shadow, God is with us." If it feels overwhelming to try to bring holy words to this unholy and devastating event, follow the advice shared for the children's time: be honest, simple, and fully present. Make space for the expression of lament, for all the strong and hard emotions this tragedy has brought forth. Resist trying to explain what God's plan or purpose might be in what happened. This is a season for questions, for making space to ponder them, and for waiting for the Mystery of God's work to unfold in due time.

After violence, there is a temptation to move away from what is painful and from questions that are impossible to answer. For some pastoral leaders, preaching about gun control or mental health reform, and crying out for justice feels timely and purposeful. It is, but not on the first Sunday. For everything there is a season, and this is a time to weep. Other preachers will be tempted to focus on matters of redemption through forgiveness. Do not move the congregation too swiftly toward forgiveness of the perpetrator. People need time to absorb the hurt and process losses before approaching the work of forgiving. There will be time for that struggle later. In the theological section that closes this chapter, further attention is devoted to the challenge of forgiveness after trauma. The preacher's words need to be pastoral. They should be spacious, making room for difficult emotions and hard questions. They should comfort and reassure. They will model for the people ways that they can do the work of lament faithfully, serve the wounded community, and be sustained by one another and by God's presence while doing so.

The Second Hymn, whether placed before the sermon or following, invites the people as they listen and respond to Scripture and the Word proclaimed to add their own silent "words" of wondering and wandering into the unfolding meaning of the event and its implications for faith. A minor key, a slower pace, and melodies that are easy to follow will be useful here. Music, heard and sung, accesses and activates parts of the brain that the spoken word cannot. Singing creates pathways, for emotional processing and for expression, that are important following trauma. Hymns accompanying Scripture and the proclamation of the Word might express questions of faith, or set a tone of faithful exploration into troubled seasons. They might reinforce the work of lament, evoke a longing for justice, or invite a commitment to be open to the journey through the wilderness, accompanying those whose path is particularly difficult.

This may be a good place for a Taizé[1] song or another simple, repetitive chorus that can act as sung prayer and as centering music, grounding worshipers while a word from God works its way into the hearts and minds of the congregation.

Letting Begin: Living into the Work of Lament and Healing

The third movement of the liturgy is response to the Word and sending, or returning to service in the world. These are important movements for God's people after trauma. Members of the congregation will be going back into a community that has been wounded by violence. They will be in pain themselves, and they will want to help others. They need to be empowered to go as wounded healers, and equipped with spiritual resources that will enable them to stay present in a place of emotional challenge and through days of disorientation and sadness.

Prayers of the People and the Lord's Prayer. A bidding prayer, which invites brief congregational voicing of expressions of need, intercession, thanksgiving, and grief, guided by the pastoral prayer framework, helps underscore the communal process of lament. Generous spaces for silence in the midst of these prayers are good, as people silently express feelings too deep for human expression (see Rom. 8:26).

The lighting of small tea candles on the table during this prayer may add visual power to the act of prayer; depending on the size and style of the congregation, members could be invited to come forward, or an acolyte or liturgist could light the candles as prayers are voiced.

Closing Hymn. The closing hymn is not about resolution of the trauma, but sounds a note of reassurance and praise as it supports trust in the work of the Spirit in their midst. As the people prepare to leave worship, the hymn should invoke and claim the comfort of the divine presence and make space for a healing process to begin, among and through the people of God.

Service Music and Anthems. The mood set by the service music—prelude, offertory, and postlude—will help support and shape the important messages of comfort and resilience after trauma. Music in a minor key can evoke and express the sorrow of the people. There should be a balance between minor and major keys, and around the pacing of the hymns, so that the mood of the music is not too heavy or ponderous. Music that is structured and feels strong (not necessarily triumphal) can help reassure the faith community and build courage to face a hard season.

"Those who sing, pray twice," said St. Augustine. The presiding pastor should work closely with the music and choir directors to select the best message, mood, and placement for the anthems chosen for this day. Choir directors may want to change the anthem to support the spiritual and emotional flow of the service, and to help both choir and congregation express their feelings.

Should Communion be served at this service? Many traditions do not celebrate the Eucharist weekly. Adding the celebration of the Lord's Supper is worth consideration. The gifts of the bread of life and the cup of salvation, made through the offering of Christ's life, are powerful redemptive metaphors in a community after trauma, when life has been lost and innocent blood spilled. The church's unity when gathered at the common Table, the table of life, is also a powerful healing image and symbolic action. Other worship leaders may feel that the additional time required to incorporate the Lord's Supper into a service that is already emotionally full is demanding too much when people are tired and stressed. Consider the congregational mood and energy in order to decide.

Informal or Contemporary Services

As in the traditional service above, consider the service as a walk through the valley of the shadow in three movements:

> *Letting Go* (we release what was and seek sanctuary in the presence of God)
> *Letting Be* (we are present to God and to one another in the midst of distress)
> *Letting Begin* (our walk and work in the valley of the shadow begins)

When people enter the service this morning, their usual feeling of joyful, energized praise will be tempered by the impact of the event on the community's heart and soul. The songs that provide the setting for the praise service this morning can help comfort, question, reassure, and offer praise to the God who is with God's people, even and especially in times of trouble. The flow of this service is part of an unfolding story of shock, anger, grief, and loss, punctuated by moments of human comfort and Holy Love. As the pastor and praise team create the flow of the music for this service, imagine entering the home of someone who has unexpectedly lost a member of their family, embracing them strongly as they cry, and then sitting beside them, maybe even in silence, bearing witness both to pain and to the comforting presence of God. Suggested songs for this service are listed in appendix 7.

In the welcome, acknowledge with love and honesty all that is in the room: the event that has changed everything, a people filled with many confused and conflicting emotions, a church that is the good and right place for lament, a God able to be present in the valley of the shadow.

The ritual of friendship and sharing the peace is more important today than ever before. Leave lots of time for tears and embracing, and have the praise band underscore this time with a song of comfort and friendship and love.

As the people bring their prayers, leave open space between what is spoken. Consider lighting small candles for each petition, or inviting the people to do so. Let this time be a spacious invitation to pray for all who are hurt and affected by the tragedy, to seek comfort and hope, to express our voice of lament. Music that underscores the prayers of the people can be calming and reassuring.

THEOLOGY IN THE AFTERMATH OF VIOLENCE

There was a murder and suicide on the church property in a large suburban congregation that took the lives of two congregation members and a member of the youth group. A few weeks after the tragedy, during the season of Lent, the senior pastor, Sarah Sarchet Butter, shared from the pulpit a powerful theological shift that had occurred within her since the trauma. Growing up in a traditional congregation that had the same pastor for over thirty years, she had memorized and recited the Apostles' Creed every Sunday, but with one omission: "He descended into hell." The longtime pastor did not believe that Jesus had descended into hell, and had personally marked out that line in every hymnbook the congregation owned. She shared that, having never affirmed Jesus' descent into hell during her Sunday school years, she felt no need to incorporate that affirmation into her own pastoral theology when she was ordained. "Until today," she said, "when I realized that since the tragedy, this congregation has descended into hell. And if we have had to go down into hell, it is comforting to know that Jesus has been there before us, and can show us the way out." It was a powerful intuitive shift, revealed through the experience of trauma, that made the story of the death and resurrection of Jesus deeply personal and real, not just for that season, but for the many seasons of pastoral care that lay ahead.

Just as the preacher and presider's task is to allow Scripture and ritual practice to support a congregation through worship, the pastor's task is to shepherd and frame the congregation's theological response as it re-forms foundational identity and practice moving forward. As described in the first chapter, often the first response to violence among the congregation or community is an adrenaline-fueled heroism. In the face of abject terror, the desire to exert normalcy and control in a situation runs high. Phrases like, "We won't let this change anything," "Let's keep Sunday just as we had planned," and "Our hope is in the Lord!" are on the lips, hearts, and minds of many who find themselves in the valley of the shadow of death, and trying to deny it. Yet such expressions more frequently express a reactive avoidance of the pain that is found in the valley of the shadow rather than a faithful proclamation that bears witness to the truth of what it is that has happened in this place (see Joel 1:2).

In an exuberant effort to proclaim "We will overcome" or "We must forgive," many faith leaders, in response to the trauma of violence, move too quickly toward words of comfort, hope, forgiveness, and reconciliation. In so doing, they ignore the pain and hurt, the rip in the fabric of life, the taste of tears shed in disbelief and anger. There are many different ways to frame a theological response to human-caused violence. Some reaffirm what was before; some, like the pastor in the story above, make a courageous leap of faith and are transformed. The reflections in the remaining pages of this chapter are personal, growing out of the observations of pastors who have led congregations through the aftermath of public violence; and also professional, reflecting on years of experience as responders in a variety of human-caused disasters. They are contextual practical theology, not meant to be prescriptive, but as a companionable guide from fellow travelers through the valley of the shadow of death.

Slow Down in the Valley

A pastor who serves as a volunteer supporting faith communities after human-caused disasters recalled his years as a pre-med student in college. He had volunteered on Sunday nights in the emergency room of a local children's hospital. "One night, the resident on duty said there would be a case coming in, a head laceration, and he wanted me to go get six bottles of saline. I obviously gave him a look that said, 'Really? Six bottles?' because he said, 'This cut will look bad, lots of blood, but it is only superficial. The danger with this type of injury is closing it up too soon. We need to wash it out, take our time, and then, after all six bottles, we'll close it up.' Years later, as I was wondering what to say on the first Sunday after a gunman killed five people in my community, including the husband of a colleague on the church staff, this story came to me: slow down, wash it out; there is danger in closing this up too soon." When confronted by unimagined evil and grief, anger and bewilderment, the advice of this resident is still good.

It may seem counterintuitive to Christians: slow down, and don't offer too much hope at the beginning. Immediately after an event, particularly on the first Sunday after something horrible has happened in a community, preachers and leaders of worship are encouraged to make space for the hurt. The energy and weight of a murder, rape, suicide, mass shooting, or other trauma is overwhelming. It is for this reason that these events are described as "human-caused disasters," since a disaster, by definition, is that which temporarily overwhelms a system's resources to cope. In the immediate aftermath of a human-caused disaster, slow way down, especially theologically. There will be a time for hope and joy. But in the immediate aftermath of community-wide trauma, it is lament—the faithful expression of anger and disbelief at the ways of the world—that might be more helpful for the congregation.

This mirrors the invitation of the Twenty-third Psalm, which is such a strong metaphor for the journey through trauma: there is a need to *walk* through the valley of the shadow of death. The instinct is to avoid the valley, or to run through it and to get beyond the "shadow of death" as quickly as possible. Yet the psalmist reminds us we are to walk *through* the valley—a slow, deliberate journey through the very places that make us afraid. The presence of the Lord reassures us along this journey, but God does not "save" us from making this trek. We cannot go back and undo the human-caused disaster; violence and trauma are now a part of our landscape. Pastors and congregations who enter this strange landscape are invited to slow down, to let the pain come out, and to walk through the valley of the shadow of death gently—leading others to do the same. It will probably take years for the energy of a traumatic event to fully dissipate. There will be time to offer hope, and peace, and love in celebratory ways. In the early stages of human-caused disaster response, lament and a compassionate presence may be the best options to offer others.

Take Time to Lament

When public violence or trauma disrupts the world, the belief that we are safe and whole because God is blessing us is abruptly and horrifically challenged. A movement into lament begins when believers are exiled from this place of settled blessing; it is initiated by a world-shattering experience that Walter Brueggemann, in his small commentary *The Message of the Psalms,* called a "movement of dismantling:"

> One move we make is *out of a settled orientation into a season of disorientation.* This move is experienced partly as changed circumstance, but it is much more a personal awareness and acknowledgment of the changed circumstance. . . . It constitutes a dismantling of the

old, known world and a relinquishment of safe, reliable confidence in God's good creation.[2]

While some faith communities consider lament an act of unfaith, a denial of the power of God or Jesus to triumph over chaos or disaster, lament is a critical engagement of a people whose world and faith assumptions have been shattered by an act of violence. Through no choice of our own, chaos has overtaken us. Though we wish God would fix it, and Jesus could carry our burden for us, there is no help for it; the only way beyond the valley of the shadow is through it, as one pastor said. In a pastoral reflection group led by responders following a community shooting, one pastor quoted Psalm 137:4: "How can we sing the Lord's song in a foreign land?" Then the pastor said,

> I get this, the rage, the helplessness that only lament can bring to speech. I remember how this feeling overwhelmed me late in the week following September 11, 2001, when my fourteen-year-old daughter turned away from the images on CNN that had been burning themselves into our souls for days, looked at me with a deep grief and weariness beyond her years, and said, "This wasn't supposed to happen in my lifetime."

"This wasn't supposed to happen." This is the heart of the complaint that fuels the psalms of lament. Through violence, that world becomes threatening, deteriorating, and incoherent. There is an anguished longing that faith should keep that "sacred space" inviolate, a place where God's good order can still be affirmed and maintained. Yet, just as the world is not like that, so the life of the church, embedded and incarnate as it is in the world, is not like that either. Brokenness, crisis, and change are as much a part of the church's life as they are a part of life in the world, whether people of faith will admit it or not. Lament is the way we mourn the failure of the world and the God we once trusted, and find our way into the faith-language of bewilderment, anger, loss, and grief. To find courage to embrace the necessity of lament is a primary task of the church after a human-caused disaster, especially because the voice of lament utilizes strong language, expressing negative emotions in ways that many of us have been schooled are inappropriate or even unfaithful.

Brueggemann says that this is why the church has failed to employ the psalms of lament in worship and proclamation:

> Serious religious use of the lament psalms has been minimal because we have believed that faith does not mean to acknowledge and

embrace negativity. We have thought that acknowledgment of negativity was somehow an act of unfaith, as though the very speech about it conceded too much about God's "loss of control." . . .

No wonder the church has intuitively avoided these psalms. They lead us into dangerous acknowledgment of how life really is . . . into the presence of God where everything is not polite and civil. They cause us to think unthinkable thoughts and utter unutterable words. Perhaps worst, they lead us away from the comfortable religious claims of "modernity" in which everything is managed and controlled.[3]

The "movement of dismantling" required of those who would honestly admit and utter the crushing negativities of faith and life is a movement of great courage and faith. Such expressions include anger, grief, pain, and bewilderment; difficult emotions to express, as revealed in Psalm 137:

> By the rivers of Babylon—
>   there we sat down and there we wept
>   when we remembered Zion.
> On the willows there
>   we hung up our harps.
> For there our captors
>   asked us for songs,
> and our tormentors asked for mirth, saying,
>   "Sing us one of the songs of Zion!"
>
> How could we sing the LORD's song
>   in a foreign land?
> . . . .
> O daughter Babylon, you devastator!
>   Happy shall they be who pay you back
>   what you have done to us!
> Happy shall they be who take your little ones
>   and dash them against the rock!

Those who find their world view "dismantled" by violence and trauma may experience a sense of abandonment and despair as profound as Jesus' words from the cross: "My God, my God, why have you forsaken me?" (Matt. 27:46; Mark 15:34; see Ps. 22:1). If they find the courage to embrace the language of lament and welcome the company of strangers in the Psalms and elsewhere who have articulated that dark place for us, the sense of the absence of God may yield to a troubling, uncertain presence. Like the whirlwind out of which God spoke to Job—Job, who had the temerity to reject easy answers and explanations for violence and suffering rooted in personal brokenness and sin—the God we discover after the affront of violence and loss may be a dangerous Stranger. In the world of lament, we learn to speak truth into the whirlwind, we lift our cries above its howling moans, and we weep until there are no more tears. With Job we say:

> Today again my complaint is bitter;
> My strength is spent on account of my groaning.
> Would that I knew how to reach Him,
> How to get to His dwelling-place.
> I would set out my case before Him
> And fill my mouth with arguments.
> I would learn what answers He had for me
> And know how He would reply to me.
> Would He contend with me overbearingly?
> Surely He would not accuse me!
> There the upright would be cleared by Him,
> And I would escape forever from my judge.
>
> But if I go East—He is not there;
> West—I still do not perceive Him;
> North—since He is concealed, I do not behold Him;
> South—He is hidden, and I cannot see Him.[4]

As we voice our complaints and demand the presence of God along the path of that difficult journey, the psalms of lament are an expression of bold faith:

> That the world is *not morally coherent*, but there is a deep incongruity in which we live, that we need neither to resolve, explain, or deny. A raw, ragged openness is linked to the awesome reality of God's holiness.[5]

Be a Compassionate Presence

One of the most striking words in the New Testament is σπλαγχνίζομαι —*splanchnizomai*—compassion. In Greek class in seminary we learned it meant "shaking guts." The Latin is *com* + *passio* or "with suffering" or "to suffer with." To have compassion for someone or a situation is to suffer with them, to allow your guts to shake in disbelief, hurt, anger, and confusion. The invitation is to not immediately try to fix them, help them, or make them feel better. A compassionate presence enters into the suffering of others gently, attentive to the disruption of a traumatic event.

It also means to be gentle with yourself if you find your guts shaking. If you are a pastoral caregiver entering the aftermath of public violence, read through the Twenty-third Psalm in anticipation of being present to those still reeling from a mass shooting event or other violence. Read the verse, "Yea, though I walk through the valley of the shadow of death, I will fear no evil: for thou art with me; thy rod and thy staff they comfort me" (v. 4 KJV). Be grateful, and accept the invitation to become the comforting companion in someone else's dark valley.

While showing up is often considered to be nine-tenths of the job, in trauma response, it is the *quality* of showing up that is most important. Trauma is disruptive to the rhythms of life and destroys any sense of normalcy. The invitation of Psalm 23 is to walk gently with oneself and others. Rather than responding like a crime-fighting superhero, a gentler, calmer, more reflective presence is helpful. While the actual experiences of trauma seem to unfold in slow motion, pastoral responses (at times) seem to move at warp speed. There is so much to do, so many people to check on, so much we need to maintain, so much we need to plan; work multiplies exactly at the time when we need to cultivate space and slow way down. Some time after a community-wide shooting near his church, the pastor, who also had lost members in the violence, reflected on his own response to the urgency of trauma:

> I can remember that the day after the shooting, we needed to change our Sunday morning worship, change the Sunday school curriculum, plan a prayer service, plan a memorial service, deal with the media and protesters, care for a grieving widow, care for each other on staff, organize a debriefing session for the congregation—the tasks multiplied faster than I could keep up with them. As I began to feel overwhelmed, a colleague stopped by my office, and after some small talk, asked: "What's the one thing you need to do next?" One thing? There are one hundred things that need to get done! But as I sat with the question, I knew the answer: I need to write Sunday's sermon. I need to get quiet and listen to the Spirit, so I went home. In the midst of a hundred things to do at church, I went home. I went home and cried and prayed and read scripture and asked the question: "What do I say about this? What do you say about this?" I gave myself the space I needed to do the work God was inviting me to do in that moment.

This is some of what it looks like offering a compassionate presence: a friend showing up or an overwhelmed pastor going home in the face of an avalanche of tasks. An invitation following trauma is for pastors to be compassionate with themselves and everyone they meet. Be compassionate in preaching, teaching, and leadership. Be compassionate with the members of the congregation. Be compassionate, period.

Trust that Christ Is Near

Often, in the midst of responding to a traumatic event, pastoral leaders want to offer hope that everything will be okay. It is a natural instinct to try and restore order in the midst of chaos. Everyone wants to get back to how things were before the arson fire or sexual assault as quickly as possible. There is a lesson to be received from Mary Magdalene at the end of the Gospel of John.

Neither Mary nor the disciples immediately recognized the presence of their beloved, resurrected friend Jesus. Mary stood weeping at the entrance of the tomb after running back to tell the disciples the horrible news that the tomb was empty. She was beside herself with grief, confused as to the facts, frantically searching for the answers as to where her friend had been taken. All that time, Jesus was near her, beside her, yet unrecognized or "disguised" as a gardener. This is an important lesson for surviving or responding to trauma: Jesus is often near *and* disguised. So, rather than proclaim the triumphant good news of Jesus Christ in the immediate aftermath of a traumatic event, rather than pronounce that all will be well soon, the invitation of Mary Magdalene is to trust that Jesus is near but unrecognized. The task for a religious leader or responder is to not identify the presence of Jesus Christ too quickly. Be Mary Magdalene. Look around. Weep. Talk to people; listen to people. Tell the stories of what happened. And let Jesus show up unexpectedly—the promise of new life not yet recognized.

Forgiving "those who sin against us"

In a reflection group with adults who had survived sexual abuse by their childhood pastor, a man spoke of his years in therapy and his ongoing struggle to forgive the perpetrator. He said, "I know that as a Christian I am supposed to forgive those who sin against me. I believe that my spiritual health depends on this. As a pastor myself, I urge others to forgive.

I tell them, and I tell myself, 'When our Lord Jesus was on the cross, he forgave his torturers, and we should do the same.' But . . . I just . . . can't." He buried his face in his hands and the room was quiet.

After a few moments, another member of the group said, "Wait a minute . . . what did Jesus say from the cross, exactly?"

Another opened the Bible and read: "Father, forgive them, for they don't know what they are doing."

"Father, forgive them," the second voice repeated. "It doesn't say, 'I forgive you' at all! It says: 'Father, forgive them'! Is it possible that Jesus prayed for God to forgive the perpetrators because he himself, still suffering and human, was not yet able to do so?"

Years later, the pastor who had survived the abuse ran into a colleague from the group at the church and said that the reframing of Jesus' prayer from the cross that day had broken open a place of hope and possibility for him, so that he had at last been able to fully experience the anger and betrayal he had carried, and then finally, put the past behind him, and be at peace. He said trying to forgive without going through the pain was what kept him stuck in the trauma for so many years.

One of the core Christian values is forgiving those who sin against us. Jesus taught it and practiced it, and most people of faith feel they want to, and *should* forgive, even if the evil done was monstrous.

For most of us, forgiveness is not so much an act of will shaped by intention and practice as it is a process, rooted in relationship, that *in time* brings reconciliation and peace. An exhortation for forgiveness, when imposed too quickly by well-intentioned faith leaders, shortcircuits the work of lament and impedes the psychological work of grieving. In the psalms of David, words of rage, anger, and vindictiveness are given full voice, *even as* the psalmist prays for grace, for peace and for restoration. Think of the powerful words of Psalm 137: "By the rivers of Babylon—there we sat down and there we wept when we remembered Zion. . . . How could we sing the LORD's song in a foreign land?" The power and beauty of that song of yearning close with this sentence, addressed to the perpetrator of exile, Babylon: "Happy shall they be who take your little ones and dash them against the rock!" Expressing angry, vengeful feelings in a prayerful context is an act of honesty and deep faith. If forgiveness for the perpetrator is something people try to work on *now*, at the beginning of living through its impact, go slowly: forgiveness is a process, and until the impact of the loss and offense has been lived into, pushing the closure of forgiveness may stunt the process of grieving.

There will always be compelling examples of communities or

individuals that act to embrace forgiveness early in the aftermath of violence. From the outside, we don't know whether that forgiveness is a fully realized expression of reconciliation, or might be more an act of hopeful intention for the future. The Old Order Amish congregation of Nickel Mines, Pennsylvania, who embraced the family of the shooter and proclaimed immediate forgiveness of his deeds within days of the shooting of their schoolchildren in October 2006, lived in close-knit intentional community with a strong theological ethic of nonviolence. After church members were gunned down on June 17, 2015, during Bible study at Mother Emanuel Church in Charleston, South Carolina, some of their family members were present and spoke at the arraignment of the shooter the very next day, offering forgiveness and commending the shooter to the judgment and mercy of God. This was a response arising from within a community whose character and resilience were forged in the aftermath of slavery and in the violence of the civil rights movement. There is no question that these demonstrations of faith and grace in the face of unspeakable violence express a deep-seated trust in the transforming power and mercy of God. At the same time, no one knows how that public intention was realized in the hearts and souls of those survivors, and at what cost. Go slowly through the valley of the shadow, and take whatever time is needed. Forgiveness is a gift of God, shaped by intention, but ultimately brought to fruition by the Holy Spirit in God's time, not our own.

3

Transitions

The introduction of this book told about a public violent event in a church in Idaho that impacted the congregation. A shooter took refuge in the church building, killed the caretaker, shot at citizens from a second-story Sunday school room, and finally killed himself in the sanctuary. Late in the first week following the shooting—when the church property was still surrounded by police crime-scene tape—parents in the church shared with elders that some of their children were having nightmares, and expressing fear of returning to the church building. They wondered whether the shooter was still present, and feared that he might attack them or their parents if they returned to church and Sunday school. The parents wondered whether their way of helping the children was right, and what they should say about the church building and Sunday school. The pastor and church leaders decided to invite trauma responders, a local child psychologist, and the Sunday school teachers and parents to a special gathering to address the questions and concerns, and to support the families. They met at a familiar community center that was popular with families in the church. Caregivers were brought in to play with the kids, and art activities and snacks were provided. With the parents and Sunday school teachers, the pastor and resource persons worked through what had happened, shared information about the church building and its repair and return to congregational use, and figured out together what might be shared with the children. There was a brief conversation about the effects of trauma in children, and parents were given resource sheets to help them support their kids. Together, the group worked out a process for reentry that would involve a ritual of cleansing, appropriate for young children, and some age-appropriate activities for each class to use as they resumed their Sunday school schedule.

The event is over. Families who have lost a loved one have been notified and their immediate needs attended to. Those hospitalized have been visited, the vigils of that first, terrible night are concluded; the gathered community has, for the time being, returned to their homes. For the moment, there is nothing left to *do*. The sun rises on a landscape that appears familiar, but everything is altered. The community, the church, its programs and its members are vulnerable in the wake of trauma. It is the responsibility of the pastoral leader to set the tone and establish a direction forward. What is needful? What is not? What's next, here in the valley of the shadow of death?

WALKING INTO THE VALLEY OF THE SHADOW

Some leaders will feel tempted to advise communities of faith to "keep calm and carry on." It may be thought that the best witness to the power of God in such circumstances is to demonstrate a strong faith that appears unaffected by violence or catastrophe. And while some ordinary practices of congregational life—worship, midweek suppers, youth gatherings, and meetings—may remain on the immediate church schedule following an event of violence, to treat those gatherings as ordinary would be a grave mistake. At least for the short term, life as we know it has been abruptly shattered. In order to honor the impact of the event on the lives of witnesses and survivors, congregational leaders should invite the community of faith to turn aside from the ordinary, to stop, and to pay attention to what is rising in their awareness. Ordinary gatherings—worship, choir practice, youth group, and the like—offer a familiar context and safe community in which people can start to tell their stories of impact and survival, and begin to weave, with their neighbors, a faith narrative, a new gospel story. As pastors, staff, and lay leadership consider the congregation's life together in the days following a violent event, each meeting, gathering, and worship event should be viewed through the lens of trauma and its power to impact individual lives and life together.

WHAT NOW?

After pastors, staff, and congregational leaders have tended to their own and their family's immediate needs and safety following a violent event, gather at the earliest opportunity to assess the needs of the congregation and its members in the aftermath. Congregations that have within their membership circles professionals with expertise in medical and psycho-social care may want to invite those professionals to participate in an expanded leadership group for the purposes of supporting members as they begin working through the trauma. Congregations differ widely in size, style, and capacity. Some may prefer to talk about what happened and share the impact on themselves and others in the congregation in a setting that involves worship, while others may find an informal setting, like a fellowship meal or small group, better. For some, a structured process may help; for others, ways of telling their story and sorting out next steps may happen more naturally. Here are some questions for leaders to keep in mind as the congregation and its smaller groups gather in the weeks following an act of public violence.

—How are we doing?

—Who are the people who will attend this gathering (Bible study, women's group, book group, youth gathering) or service?

—Who are their trusted leaders?

—Who among them may be most deeply impacted by the event?

—What will good spiritual and emotional care after trauma look like within the context of this group's customary practices?

—Who (among skilled and stable church leadership and staff) is available and has the necessary connections and skills to support this first meeting?

—Following each gathering, are there any signs of unusual distress, people whose response to trauma may need special follow-up, or insights that should be captured and shared? Who is missing?

We continue the story of the small congregation that witnessed the shooting of their organist during morning worship (see chapter 1). At the conclusion of the evening gathering where the congregation had shared their experiences of the murder, conversation turned to the few people who were not present, and what could or should be done to reach out to them. They asked questions about where worship would be next week, whether a funeral had been scheduled. The pastor promised to sort that out with leadership, and get back to everyone in a day or so. At the end of the meal, as some of the older folks began to gather their things to go home, a few of the elders sat down and, feeling that they wanted to begin to look at next steps, made a few simple assignments regarding people to be checked on and actions needed to see to arranging worship at the yoked Lutheran church for the next few Sundays. They agreed to meet again in a couple of days, and to keep in closer touch than usual in between. They made no long-term or important decisions that evening, but simply tended to what needed to happen next and figured out who would do what. The community and congregation were small enough that this informal process was a healthy way for them to begin the work of integrating the tragedy and its impact on the community and congregation.

CHECK IN WITH STAFF AND LEADERS

It is vital that the staff and church leaders who share responsibility for supporting the well-being of the congregation following a traumatic event are themselves supported, and have adequate opportunities to work through their own experiences and feelings. Listening to the stories of others exposes leaders and pastoral caregivers to the possibility of secondary traumatic stress (becoming affected by hearing and reacting to the trauma narratives of others). In order to keep staff and congregational leaders spiritually resilient while supporting others, regular check-ins are important. During the first few weeks after a traumatic event, do these check-ins at each gathering of leaders and staff. Doing this supports the spiritual resilience and recovery of leaders, and also models good pastoral caregiving processes for the general congregation.

A Check-In Process

—Open with prayer and quiet, inviting those present to identify places of tension in their bodies and to relax those places. Telling a traumatic story in a tense body does not support healing and integration but reinforces the pain and stress of the event. Those who speak should be mindful of keeping their own bodies relaxed while sharing; those listening should relax their bodies as well. Deep breathing, breathing from the diaphragm, and intentionally relaxing a muscle group that holds tension are all ways to do this. If it becomes apparent that stress is escalating as members of the group share, relax your body and remind others to do so. Take time to breathe and be.

—Invite each person present to *briefly* describe how they are feeling and doing. Some may choose not to share; that is perfectly acceptable. Suggest that each one's comments should focus on that person's own response to the event and present state of being; they might be encouraged to respond to these questions: What do you notice about this event and its impact on you? What do you feel?

—Keep it brief and focused; it should not devolve into an attempt to make a coherent group narrative, correct facts or impressions, or solve problems. Others in the group should not interrupt, critique, or "fix" what is being expressed; this is each person's holy ground of experience, memory, and feeling response. Appreciative and attentive listening should shape this time.

—When all have had a chance to speak, ask whether any who previously declined wish to speak at this time; if not, invite a minute of silence to honor what has been spoken and felt.

—Another brief prayer to conclude this time may express thanksgiving for those gathered and their stories, then offer all that has been expressed, spoken or unspoken, into God's keeping.

This process, or a shorter version of it, may need to be engaged more than once. It may be helpful for the first few weeks to have a brief time of checking in around the continuing unfolding of the aftermath; also, to model "checking in" on those ordinary joys and concerns of each person's life. In time, expressions centered on the traumatic event will shift in intensity, diminish, and eventually yield entirely to more ordinary matters. This is a natural progression, and care should be taken not to force focus back onto the event when the emerging healing process shifts attention back to the everyday.

Worship

The centrality of worship to the work of lament, and the processes of healing, supporting, and meaning-making in a congregation following trauma cannot be overstated. Special worship gatherings—vigils, candlelight services, labyrinth walks, services for wholeness and healing, memorial services and funerals—are vital ways the congregation can connect for lament, mutual support, and self-care. Worship remains the heart of a congregation's life and the primary locus of its narrative, and will be therefore the liturgical centerpiece of the community's "service of worship." That is, worship is the place where the work of lament, the grieving of losses, and the expressions of anger and hope are held in holy tenderness. Worship is where the community begins the challenging work of making sense of what has happened and sows the fragile seeds of hope, so that resilience may grow and restoration to wholeness bears fruit. The liturgy and rituals of the faith hold the story of the congregation together and provide the creative form that broods over brokenness and brings healing shape to the chaos of trauma and its aftermath.

Meetings and Recurring Events

At some point when things slow down a little, it may be helpful to look at events scheduled for the congregation in the near future. Are there events that should be cancelled or postponed, because they are inappropriate in the wake of violence, irrelevant in the immediate moment, or not possible because the participants are too affected or the site of the event was compromised? Are there new gatherings to be substituted in their place?

Organizing Follow-Up

A board or newsprint may be used to visualize the community and capture the most urgent needs. Church directories and the church calendar for the week will be helpful. Start from the center (the closest impact to the trauma event) and work outward. Working together, identify people, families, and groups whose closeness to the trauma, to a victim or survivor, may make their need for support more acute: Who are the people most immediately affected by this event? Survivors? The perpetrator and his/her family and friends? Family members and close friends of victims and survivors? Witnesses to the event? Are there people in the hospital or who are dealing with the loss of a loved one? Are they being accompanied appropriately at this time? Follow up, and then keep following up.

Next, gather the names of those who may have self-identified as desiring additional support through phone calls, texts, comments, or notes communicated to anyone in leadership. Have someone carefully check the church's social media sites and email. Assign people to follow up. Each congregation has members who have particular vulnerabilities and needs; trauma may exacerbate those vulnerabilities. Sunday school teachers, for example, may benefit from meeting prior to the first Sunday after an event to share their own concerns and wisdom and receive insights into helpful strategies for children and youth after a traumatic event. A follow-up session with those leaders to assess how their group is doing will be helpful, both in terms of continuing to take the temperature of the congregation and in supporting those leaders. Check in, and follow up.

Mass violence events, even those with no direct involvement of the congregation or its members, may have significant impact on particular groups within a congregation. A school or college shooting will particularly impact children, youth, and young adult groups, their families, and their teachers and leaders, for example. Think about who was involved in the event: are there significant connections to persons or groups within the congregation? For example, no congregation member's child may have been a victim of a catastrophic school bus crash, but children in the church may have close friends who were, or a Boy Scout troop that meets in the church might have lost a member. These groups may desire support from the church community, and their leadership may have additional resources for supporting healing and resilience in the community of faith.

Be Present and Make Space

Sometimes, just knowing that space has been set aside, physically and spiritually, for members of the community to talk about their feelings and the event with a trusted pastor, counselor, or friend is enough. Just because a large group doesn't show up for a planned event doesn't mean it isn't important for them to know that the space is being held, in a holy way, for those who may need it. In one congregation, after a mass shooting at the nearby college, pastors and faculty believed that many people wanted a chance to talk anonymously to a professional/pastoral caregiver. They said the group process worked for some, but not for all of the members of the community, so they asked that national response team members spend the morning in a nearby Starbucks, and then join a group in the faculty lounge for a communal lunch with others, following. They made that availability known to members of the congregation, campus ministry, and faculty. Three responders sat for several hours, drinking coffee at Starbucks, and no one came. One of the responders expressed frustration that the morning had been wasted. But at lunch with the larger group, many showed up and expressed their appreciation that responders were there *and also* that there had been a space and a time reserved for those who needed it that morning. Though no one came, just holding that space sacred was a part of the healing process. As the poet John Milton concluded in his sonnet "When I consider how my light is spent . . . / They also serve who only stand and wait."[1]

In the next chapter, we turn our attention to the season of disillusionment that follows as the community of faith continues to walk more deeply into the valley of the shadow in the continuing aftermath of violence and trauma.

4

Phase Two: Disillusionment

At the height of the war in Syria, pastors from the region came together in Beirut for a consultation on pastoral care during times of war and trauma. During a biblical reflection around Psalm 137, they considered what captured their attention. Some spoke of the deep sadness in the text, the sense of hopelessness and loss and grief. Others spoke of the hateful offense of causing the exiles to sing their homeland songs in "a strange land" for the entertainment of their captors . . . how deep their bitterness must be to be forced to do such a thing. Others described how this psalm expressed a desire for revenge against enemies. A pastor from Syria spoke about a prayer meeting he attended with several other pastors and laypeople just after a major assault on their city by the Al Nusra Front. People were praying for the safety of survivors, for protection as the attacks and bombings continued, for shelter and food for those who were refugees, for strength and faith to undertake the hard work of supporting those hurt and undertaking the rebuilding. In the midst of the prayers, one woman burst out, "May the people who did this thing be forever cursed! May what has happened to us be visited upon them also!!! May they suffer . . ." One of the pastors in the prayer group leaned over and, holding out his hand to her, said, "Hush, this is not how we pray." There was silence among the pastors in the Beirut consultation as the pastor from Aleppo looked up from his story and concluded, "But we do pray this way. Scripture shows us that this is human experience. These feelings are real."

Disillusionment *is* real. This painful phase emerges when heroic behavior dissipates. During and immediately after a crisis, heroic behavior keeps the community unified and provides a necessary, bracing antidote to the horror of violence. But like a rush of adrenaline, heroism is unsustainable for the long haul. In its wake, disillusionment rises with its loss of belief, faith, and trust. Disillusionment evokes negative emotions that once seemed distant from the life of faith. The community and its members struggle as feelings of rage, hatred, vengeance, and hopelessness displace joy, peace, and purpose. Within faith communities, disillusionment often feels stagnating and spiritless, as if the congregation has slowly ground to a halt.

Part of the work of this phase is to prepare individuals as well as the congregation to be open to the process of disillusionment and to begin walking, however slowly, through the valley of the shadow of death. Acceptance is painful. Leadership in this season requires accepting a new reality and learning how to function after traumatic experience. This work involves discovering a new identity, one that has been altered due to the trauma or violence. It is walking into the pain rather than walking away from it. It is finding new ways to be productive rather than disengaged. It is discovering meaning, embodying the fullness of life even while living in and with pain. This is the difficult beginning of the work of healing. It is not quick work, and it is complicated.

SPIRITUAL AND EMOTIONAL CHARACTERISTICS OF DISILLUSIONMENT

The human-caused disaster chart in the introduction (see p. xiv) shows how, after a traumatic event, a sense of heroism in the community peaks and then abruptly collapses downward into disillusionment that bottoms out in despair or something that feels just like it. As the chart indicates, there is a tipping point. At some point, there is a transition into the phase of disillusionment. For individuals, a number of variables influence transitioning into this phase. It could be fatigue, or the realization that the demands of the event outweigh the resources a pastor or congregation can offer. It could be a behavioral shift, like noticing that one has stopped ordinary habits of socializing, exercising, or other means of self-care. It might be signified by an increasing use of alcohol or medication for self-soothing, or by excessive sleep. Though most people get over being heroic naturally, there are exceptions. There may be some who demonstrate resistance to relinquishing an illusion that things will go back as before if they can just keep busy enough, or seem to enjoy the attention and affirmation received from their heroic behavior. Most people are doing the very best they can under these circumstances. It's difficult to predict when and how people transition into the disillusionment phase.

This phase can also be described as a movement into lament. Lament speaks to what lies ahead, just as laments in scripture give voice to pain and describe work that needs to take place. The theologian and biblical scholar Walter Brueggemann in his commentary *The Message of the Psalms* uses the psalms of lament to underscore the importance of the work of disillusionment, which he describes as a season of disorientation. The movement of dismantling required of congregations and their members, who in the wake of a tragic event would honestly admit and utter the negativities of faith and life, is a movement of great courage and faith. Such expressions include anger, grief, pain, and bewilderment—difficult emotions to express, as seen in Psalm 137. Brueggemann affirms the necessity for people of faith to be able to open up to what he describes as "circumstances of exile" without abandoning belief. At the same time, he acknowledges how challenging disillusionment can be and how strongly people may resist this uncomfortable descent into a spirituality marked by negativity and uncertainty.[1]

The phase of disillusionment, honest and dangerous though it may feel, is part of the process of healing—not an end in itself but an authentic pathway toward restoration and wisdom. If there is continuity in this phase, it is the painful movement through the valley of the shadow. Among individuals, emotions and energy are scattered and shifting. A loss of faith and passion is typical as idealism and hope yield to painful reality. During this phase a congregation deals with sorrow, abandonment, and listlessness. There may be emotional intensity as well as a deepening sense of despair or helplessness. The steep pitch of the line on the chart is a reminder of how sharp and abrupt this phase feels.

Despite its negative character, the phase of disillusionment is not unhealthy. Rather, it serves as a necessary corrective to denial or naive idealism, supporting the congregation in its growth toward restoration and wisdom. A season of disillusionment is necessary to grow into the truths of the experience. It is the process one goes through so that the event and its impact can be integrated. Though it is a natural progression, it is difficult, and most often is met with resistance because it means accepting that what is lost really happened and that circumstances are as bad as they feel. There is no returning to the way things were and no fixing what has been permanently altered. The community is left with the discouraging and painful reality that life will never be the same again. There is a different life forward from the way things used to be, what may be referred to as a *new normal*.

PASTORAL LEADERSHIP

Disillusionment is the most complex of the three phases. People integrate the experience of trauma and its aftermath in a wide variety of ways, and "bottom out" spiritually at differing paces, creating a challenge for the pastoral leader who is trying to effectively support congregational recovery. This phase requires adeptness with ongoing assessment, a consistent and less-anxious presence, effective communication skills, the capacity to tolerate intense emotions, and a commitment to maintain boundaries.

The process of disillusionment, while downward-trending, also bounces like an EKG of a person with an arrhythmia. Emotionally, clergy, faith leaders, and congregants are all over the place in this phase. Disillusionment takes on different characteristics: it shatters and saddens. It opens the eyes and forces survivors to perceive, interpret, and understand differently. Energy and ambition may wane, replaced by a sense of wandering without a definite aim or direction. The trend is downward and there is a bottoming out, but the process is neither linear nor precise.

Being present to and recognizing when this shift from devastation and heroism to disillusionment occurs is an art. Rather than attempting to predict the duration of time between one phase and the other, the pastoral leader should instead become attuned to changes in behaviors that occur among the variety of congregants and community members who are affected. These changes may appear as a shift from lots of energy to a lack of energy, or even a depression. Tears may come unexpectedly. People may just be quiet; there are no words. Some people may feel aimless during this phase. Where does one go while in the shadow of death? How does one proceed when there is nothing left to fix? That is why this phase can be one of the most exhausting ones as well. For the leader, this is a time when the vast array of expressions among the community and congregation may be beyond the capacities of one person to manage. Still, there are practices that have been proven to mitigate some of this exhaustion and enable clergy and congregants to keep moving forward faithfully.

Where the head goes, the body follows. A critical contributing factor for a healthy transition from the heroic phase into the disillusionment phase is when the leader or "head" makes the transition. When the leader no longer sees value or opportunity in heroic activity and shifts into disillusionment, it indicates that a transition will also occur for the community. When there is a tipping point for the pastoral leader, the focus changes, and the message is different. When this happens, the body or congregation becomes more open and willing to move as well.

Storytelling is essential. In the phase of disillusionment, this practice is more difficult than during ordinary times. While ordinarily, community members are eager to share their stories, during this season there is often resistance. Emotions and conversations are raw and intense. The trauma may have caused or uncovered diffused feelings of hostility or underlying conflict that move people toward avoidance. Counterintuitively, getting people together is more difficult than it seems. And yet traumatologists concur that narrative or storytelling about the event is one of the three necessary components in normalizing and eventually healing the effects of trauma.

It is important for the staff to gather for intentional times to talk. A practical way to encourage gathering and talking among the congregation is for the leaders to model it. Conversation should ripple outward in order to give the congregation a way to confront the experiences, lessen their symptoms, and externalize the trauma. Story sharing gives the congregation a structure and the opportunity to ritualize the experience.

The truth will make you free. Here's the tricky part. When there is a traumatic incident or violent event within a congregation, narrative is often thwarted. At best half-truth is reported, as rumor and innuendo are circulated or read in the local news reports. Have a healthy suspicion of information coming from everyone. It's usually redacted for purpose or effect. It is important that congregational leaders encourage truth-telling and guard against rumor and half-truths.

There are reasons that narrative is restricted after a trauma. There may be an ongoing criminal investigation that limits the flow of information. Perhaps the crisis management intervention protocol needs to be followed. When traumatic violence occurs within the congregational system, relationships can be compromised as feelings of guilt or expressions of blame disrupt relationships among individuals and groups. Providing pastoral care to the family of a perpetrator may be seen as in conflict with providing care to survivors, and congregants may choose sides, or press inappropriately for information as they seek to make sense of what happened. The pastor must take care to balance the value of honest narrative with the ethics of pastoral confidentiality. Even in times when narrative is stilted, conversation brings the congregation back into community. Encourage ongoing gatherings and opportunities for sharing essential narrative in safe and truthful ways.

Focus on community. "If you want to go fast, walk alone. If you want to go far, walk together." This African proverb is a reminder that after trauma, a byproduct of being in community is a new sense of orientation. Together, the community orients itself by finding a shared direction, working toward acceptance. Normalizing the violent incident requires this; acceptance is the expected outcome in this phase, and without it the work of restoration cannot begin. The trauma occurred, and nostalgic yearnings to return back to life as it was *before* will not be fulfilled. Trauma cannot be erased. If denial is seen as refusing to acknowledge a situation, avoiding facing the facts, and minimizing the consequences of the incident, then the work of acceptance should be understood as the opposite. Regardless of how incomprehensible the event—such as the shootings at Sandy Hook Elementary or the murder of the church organist during a morning worship service—acceptance requires acknowledging the situation, facing the facts, and witnessing to the impact and consequences it has in survivors' lives and in the life of the community. Some of the work of accepting comes naturally. People are generally resilient, and, given the necessary resources, accept and begin the work of integrating the trauma into their lives and worldviews. Time does not heal all wounds, but it does help most survivors grow into the truths of the experience.

Practice appreciative inquiry. Asking some key questions during this phase may provide pastoral leaders with a deeper awareness of what is happening in the life of the congregation during this challenging season. Questions like these will be good indicators of how the process of acceptance is unfolding: Are congregants and staff members connecting with one another and building healthy relationships? Are they drawing strength from one another? Are they speaking honestly and not keeping secrets? How are local resources being utilized to support spiritual resilience and recovery? Is a sense of hope stirring? How are members taking care of themselves, and one another? Are they embracing change? What new goals are emerging? What does worship feel like these days? Sound assessments are generated by honest and open inquiry into the state of the community, so that pastors and leaders can effectively determine appropriate next steps during the congregation's passage through the valley of the shadow.

VOCATIONAL TRAUMA

Pastors and staff of religious communities impacted by violence are not immune to the effects of primary, secondary, and chronic post-traumatic stress. In fact, the impact of such events on professional leadership may be complicated and more sustained than the impact on the congregation and its members. Frequently, pastors and church staff report that they begin to feel worse just as the congregation is beginning to feel better. In some cases, pastors and staff leaders in congregations put their own grieving and processing on hold while they tend to the life of the community. They may mine their own feelings, faith struggles, and questions for examples and invitations to their parishioners, in order to facilitate community healing and recovery. Like a mother who goes hungry in order to provide food for her children, church leaders may give all they have to others, again and again, justifying their neglect of self-care by the urgency and intensity of the need in the congregation. They may be intending to nourish themselves later on, but often fail to do so until far too much time has passed. This vocational trauma can begin with the event and its immediate aftermath, but customarily, it emerges and intensifies after the initial period of heroism.

A Syrian pastor attending the consultation on trauma-informed pastoral care described earlier spoke about the changes in his own ministry: "We were not trained to deal with people outside of the range of baptizing, marrying, and so on.

"Before, preaching was an art, a part of ritual, a tool to change a small corner of the church. You preach to them in order to help people come back to right thinking. But suddenly in the crisis we are demanded to answer universal questions, difficult questions. Two days ago we saw a list of situations faced by a person in trauma. We live all of these! This crisis pushes us to try to get out of this situation, on all levels, especially spiritual. Some have moved away from God, because they are angry. They have a formula in their mind, and they are angry. Where are you, God? How are we to be? Should we exist with weapons? Should we run away? Should we be in the front line? Why are we alive? Is it to support others? If so, who? Many people in the church are angry that the church is helping the Muslims, who are the cousins of Daesh (ISIL). They feel we should only help the Christians. These questions have a bitter taste. We reach places where we are depressed, lost, without peace, down. How can we preach a message of peace when we are in need of peace? We are like Jesus in the garden: praying that God would take this away from him."

Vocational trauma can be understood as the changes that occur in the nature and sense of call of the pastor or congregation due to the effects of trauma. They may be experienced in a minimal way, such as an adjustment in the pastor's self-care regimen, or more seriously, as in a chronic loss of purpose or energy for ministry, a separation or divorce in the pastoral family, or the dissolution of a pastoral call. Vocational trauma can also impel positive changes, such as a deeper immersion in the whole life of the community, a commitment to explore some new arena of professional expertise, or a deepened commitment by the pastoral leader to spiritual formation or personal and relational self-care.

The pastoral leader holds responsibility for crafting the emerging post-traumatic story of the congregation; she leads the people's spiritual exploration through distress and chaos; counsels those whose exposure or experience is extreme; crafts, along with other staff and leaders, the way the story will be preached, framed for the general public, and lived out in the practice of the congregation. The pastoral leader gets to speak a word from God into the traumatic aftermath and reflects the congregation's words and wonderings back into the divine presence. No wonder some pastors report feeling an intensified sense of call and divine presence in the early days; then find themselves, weeks or months later, wondering why they are still in the ministry when they feel so fraudulent and empty, or more sadly, leaving the work or community they loved because they no longer have the vision or energy to sustain their identity in parish life.

The child-care center of a midsized congregation in a small city was the locus of a domestic violence event that resulted in the wounding of two children and the shooting deaths of a church member, who was school staff, and the police officer who first responded to the 911 call. The church had copastors, one of whom was away on vacation during the shooting and its immediate aftermath. The other copastor arrived on the scene immediately upon being informed of the incident, and provided pastoral care to the affected families, congregation, and the school staff. The church and neighborhood were devastated by the event, and for the following two years, ministry there was centered on recovery from the event and a deeper engagement between the child-care center and the church community.

The pastor who had been present in the aftermath of the event was deeply changed by his experience of trauma, engaging fully in leadership in the community's recovery and the re-creation of the relationship between church and school. He received support from the board of his church to begin doctoral studies in pastoral care and trauma response, and members reported that his preaching and spiritual leadership had become more profound in the wake of the disaster.

The second copastor returned after his vacation to find that the congregation's experience of trauma had created a barrier between his experience and theirs, one he found difficult to transcend. He listened attentively to members' stories and provided appropriate pastoral care, but came to feel in time that he had not "signed up" for pastoral leadership in a traumatized congregation. After a year, he began to look for a new position, and eventually left congregational ministry for a different profession.

The experience of violent events in the life of a community of faith changes and challenges the sense of calling of its leadership. It is a vital spiritual task for pastoral leaders and those who support their work and ministries to understand the ways a call changes during a season of impact following violence, and to continue to be open to changes that unfold later, when congregational life reaches a new normal. Sustaining or addressing changes to the leader's sense of call when the crisis and its aftermath are past demands attentiveness and a willingness to adapt. Pastors who are committed to a faithful engagement of this process may find it useful to work with a spiritual director, or to participate in vocational counseling. The leader may re-engage or relinquish parts of, or sometimes the entirety of, ministry, as the work following a traumatic event reaches resolution. Trauma changes individuals and systems: vocational issues that emerge in its wake need to be treated with grace and addressed with openness and compassion.

STAFF AND LAY EXPERIENCES

Generally, the intensity of the symptoms is related to the proximity of the event to members of the community: the closer the member, the stronger the traumatic response. During the disillusionment phase, symptoms vary widely. Members may intensify or reduce their levels of participation in congregational activities or worship. People who showed up for everything may drop out, temporarily or permanently. Others may commit more deeply to the life of faith, using the tragedy as a means of enriching their meaning-making and inspiring their service to God and to community.

Some members may engage in attempts to continue to process and honor the impact of the event, insisting that the tragedy remain "front and center" long after others have integrated what happened into their common life, and moved on to a place of healing. Others may drop out, or cease to find their customary joy and sense of meaning in participation. Some may aggressively resist communal rituals or memorials of the event. They may say that the life of faith is stronger than tragedy, and the church should forgive, forget, and move on as soon as possible. Since the ordinary story of the community is disrupted by the violence, and since the worship life of a community of faith is inherently narrative in nature, a sense of confusion or disconnection may be present in worship and other church activities.

Some members of the community may experience and express a sense of shame or guilt during this phase. Even though there may be no rational reason for the person to feel shame at the inability to have prevented or stopped the violence, these feelings are real and should be respected. Traumatologist Eric Gentry describes *shame* as "the placeholder for interrupted narrative due to trauma."[2] As the member learns to tell his or her story of the traumatic event and successfully reconnects the "before" story with the "after," the shame that demarks the impact of the event will abate. Though it is generally a pastor or friend's instinct to reassure, or deny the reason for feelings of shame, it is helpful to realize that such emotions are holy ground; they represent the cost of being human and fully present to even the most difficult experiences of living.

Disillusionment is often marked by community life that seems disjointed and even fragmented. Congregational systems, like individuals, experience trauma as a disruption, an abrupt break in the community's narrative, which produces disorientation and anxiety. As with individuals, the "story" of the congregation—its sense of identity or mission—may lose coherence and direction as the system struggles to make sense of the spiritual injury of a human-caused disaster. This may be described as *missional trauma*. Among congregational leaders, there will be lots of good conversation in which solutions and programs to address next steps are offered. Some suggestions will have merit, but nothing will be implemented. Other conversations will offer solutions that will be unreasonable and make no sense, and yet they will be attempted. There will be awkward quiet moments, and conversations in which little will be offered, and leaders may think of the time as having been wasted. There will be blame and guilt, anguish and anger. There will be accusations and confrontations. The fight-or-flight responses that trauma psychologists identify will sometimes be apparent among members of the congregation, as some engage and others fall away. This phase is not about fixing. It is about moving closer toward acceptance.

MISSIONAL TRAUMA

Missional trauma refers to the ways trauma and violence may impact the purpose or activities of a congregation. What seemed good, normal, and possible *before* such an event may seem meaningless, frivolous, or too much trouble *after*. Plans, practices, and mission events should be examined on a case-by-case basis, considering carefully the present moment's needs and the context of the church and community. Honoring the effect of such events means that congregational leadership should take time and care to attend to the actions and unexpected inactions that emerge in congregational life following a trauma. These changes in the pattern of common life are part of the way the community and its people are processing what happened. Trying to "get on with our mission," without respecting the impact of a traumatic event, dismisses important theological themes that are strongly held by many faith traditions. For example, the suffering, death, and descent into hell of Jesus the Christ, which is a core affirmation of Christian creeds, invites congregations who have experienced a similar journey through the valley of death to claim, and not deny, the power of that experience.

As traumatic events work their way through communal life, changes in congregational or staff priorities, cancellation or postponement of some mission or fellowship activities is normal and should be embraced. Pastoral and lay leaders will want to be permissive and generous in negotiating with committees, choirs, staff members, and established groups in the days and months following a violent event. To refuse to incorporate the cost of such events in the lives and commonwealth of a faith community is a mistake. Embracing changes in the mission of the congregation in the months following trauma demonstrates belief in the power of resurrection; not to do so is a denial of its power in the midst of death; it is a turning away from the Holy Spirit who broods over chaos and brings creation out of nothing.

ANOTHER FORM OF CONGREGATIONAL TRAUMA:
CLERGY SEXUAL MISCONDUCT

Clergy sexual misconduct is a kind of congregational trauma that creates an especially difficult context of disillusionment. Pastoral misconduct is experienced as a betrayal of individuals and community. Often, the process of moving toward acceptance through sharing narrative in community is thwarted by the absence of an identified leader willing or able to guide the congregation honestly. The natural flow of narrative, connection, orientation, and acceptance is compromised. Narrative shuts down as boundaries close between internal and external resources. Power dynamics are centralized or move toward hierarchy. Stress increases, and the system becomes more anxious, more protective and isolated. Key leadership often becomes paralyzed and polarized. When the leader/pastor is the accused perpetrator, channels of communication and trust are ruptured. The narrative shared with the congregation will then be managed by whoever is doing the leading. They control the script and determine where the energy needs to be directed.

> *After the pastor was arrested on child pornography charges, his spouse stepped into the leadership role. She took control of the information and became the sole source of communication for the congregation. She was, in fact, the person who they trusted to tell them the truth. As she expressed complete support, never wavering from suggesting anything other than the innocence of her husband, the congregation listened only to what she wanted them to hear. So there was a circling of support for their beloved pastor as well as mounting anger against the accusers and the investigating commission. The staff, key leaders, and membership were stunned when the church court removed him as their pastor and refused to believe any information gathered during the process. When, nearly a year after his arrest, the pastor negotiated a plea arrangement and went to prison, the congregation collapsed in shock.*

Congregations that experience this sort of trauma need to be supported by skilled leadership from *outside* the affected system. Honesty and compassion are essential. Clear and regular communication from those leaders are necessary elements for the congregation to effectively navigate the difficult journey through betrayal and loss. Clergy sexual misconduct, while appropriately understood and treated by supervising judicatories as a disciplinary issue, also should be viewed through the lens of trauma. Its effects on survivors and congregational systems mirror those of public violence, and the process of resolution and healing follows the same phases. There are a number of excellent books addressing the impact and processes supporting recovery from clergy sexual misconduct listed in the Suggested Readings list.

CONGREGATIONAL CARE

Congregational care during the season of disillusionment following human-caused disaster is an art requiring intentionality paired with gentleness. It demands patience and an ability to tolerate with grace a bewildering range of emotions and behaviors. Members' emotions may veer from rage and depression to denial. Some will practice detachment or demonstrate a determination to recover that is rooted in outright dismissal of the impact of the event on the life of the community. All of these responses are normal, and all of the skills and wisdom pastoral leaders possess will be employed in walking alongside this people of faith as they negotiate a safe path through the valley of the shadow of death. It can be difficult to encourage people to walk with intentionality through this important process of dismantling and loss, rather than just to hunker down and hope it will be over soon. But in this time of denial, anger, bargaining, depression, and acceptance (yes, those familiar stages of grief!), the seeds of wisdom and a deeper humanity are sown; and the congregation that has the support to engage this dismantling work well will become a more profoundly spiritual and joyous community when that work is fulfilled.

"How can we sing the LORD's song in a strange land?"
Experiencing Resistance

Some months after the university shooting that took eleven lives, a team of national disaster responders returned to the congregation that had invited them into the aftermath of the event as resource and support persons. The intent of this second visit was to "take the temperature" of the congregation and its campus ministry, support and assess the resilience and condition of the pastoral and lay leadership of the church, and to continue to help the pastor and church board lead the community faithfully through the ongoing process of integration and recovery.

They arrived at the church to some unexpected surprises. The youth house on the edge of the church grounds, where one student had died, was gone, leaving behind a patch of raw, scraped earth that looked like a wound. The demolition had occurred as the result of a decision reached by the church leadership a few weeks after the tragedy. Members had said they couldn't bear looking at the building, which reminded them of the shooting, so when one session member suggested it should be torn down, it was. Plans were in the very early stages to figure out what to do with the now empty land; it seemed that getting rid of the reminder was for this congregation the first and most important thing to do.

The national responders attended a number of regularly scheduled congregational gatherings (the women's association monthly tea, choir practice, a Sunday school teachers' meeting, and Sunday worship). They noticed a strange disconnect, evident at each gathering, from the rawness of grief expressed by the demolition of the building and the lack of interest in talking about how they were doing. Committees and groups alike reported that they were "over it" and wanted to move on with normal church life. They said they felt just fine, and were irritated by their leadership's insistence on continuing to process the tragedy communally. However, the pastor reported that church attendance was down, as was participation in youth group, the women's association, and the midweek Bible study. Some of the kids in youth group said that their parents were fighting more than usual, and all reported they felt constrained by the curtailing of freedoms and independence that parents and the youth leaders had imposed in the wake of the shooting. On Sunday morning, the congregation appeared disconnected, unresponsive, and subdued—a marked difference from their previous vibrant celebration. The pastor pulled one of the responders aside, confessing in a tone of despair that he was beginning to wonder whether it was time to move on, whether he had "lost" the call and vital relationship he had enjoyed in the seven years of ministry they had shared.

Resistance to hard experiences and unfamiliar emotions is sometimes a powerful factor in the work of disillusionment. In the laments of Scripture, this is often expressed as a longing for things to be the way they were *before*. For the household of faith, the home place of the people of God is supposed to be safe and coherent. When the world outside is threatening, deteriorating, or incoherent, responsibility devolves all the more onto the religious community to keep sacred space inviolate. Shouldn't church be, after all, a place where God's good order can be affirmed and maintained? Struggling with this expectation, congregations strive to seem normal when they feel anything but. They pretend, they avoid, they resist. They decisively remove from their scope of vision anything that reminds them of what happened, but the wound left behind still bleeds, and it will continue to do so until it is treated.

Settling In, Not Settling

The key for pastors, congregational leaders, and responders to support congregations during the difficult transition from *before* to *after* is to compassionately acknowledge that the longing for faith and life to be as they were *before* is an appropriate part of the grief process, but not an end in itself. Brokenness, crisis, challenge, and change are as much a part of the church's life as they are a part of life in the world, and a congregation living through the aftermath of public violence can come to understand this, and tolerate the discomfort and sorrow such understanding produces. This is a "cross-place" that can be named and embraced. There is no returning down the previous path, but other paths are open. The community can choose to cover up and deny, or may choose to incorporate their losses, respecting their cost.

This can be accomplished by modeling a consistent willingness to tolerate and even embrace the difficult and confusing emotions the event has engendered. Pastors should check in regularly with leaders and congregants, accepting the full range of coping strategies as part of a normal response, and weaving that range of responses into the unfolding narrative of the congregation's walk through the valley of the shadow.

As much as possible, pay attention to marker events and events outside the community, which may awaken and evoke fresh expressions of disillusionment. Examples of such events are the arrest, arraignment, trial, or sentencing of the perpetrator; funerals of those killed; the delayed death of someone previously injured in the event; "firsts" such as the first day back at the school, or in the sanctuary, the first month following the event, the first year marker. Similar events occurring in another community, especially those that garner strong national publicity, can reawaken grief and loss in fresh and unexpected ways. Events of this kind may provide an opportunity for the congregation to revisit the event and reassess how they are doing, from then until now. Each successive piece of the process is another part of the story that deserves attention and may need an avenue for expression, whether informal or otherwise, so that new understandings may emerge and healing can continue.

In worship leadership, frequent mention and processing of theological questions and communal circumstances related to the event may, as weeks and months pass, yield to less frequent expressions; but the pastoral leader needs to continue to name and evoke the work that is being done of lament, grieving, and integration.

Adult and youth who participate in Sunday school or other shared learning opportunities can also provide a setting for members and groups to walk through the valley of the shadow together and process their experience meaningfully. Congregations may want to engage in more intentional study of the Psalms, tracking their own progression through the wilderness by "listening in" on the wandering of our ancestors through seasons of exile. Offering retreats for contemplation and storytelling; respite for caregivers; and frequent, simple opportunities to connect for fellowship, sharing, and community-building are very important expressions of congregational care at this time.

Continuing the process of "checking in" with staff and congregational leadership on changed patterns of participation, unusual eruptions of distress in persons or families, or alarming symptoms of more serious "dis-ease" are important disciplines for pastors and spiritual caregivers in the period of disillusionment.

Advice to leaders in the immediate wake of a human-caused disaster is still resonant at this time: stop, pay attention, notice, and reflect on what the community is seeing, feeling, hearing, sensing. This is a cross-place: resurrection life can and will come for those who are willing to endure the cross and its cost.

At this stage of the response to a violent or traumatic event, focus shifts to providing "care to caregivers": clergy, staff, lay leaders, and community leaders. Two ways to address community-wide care and support for those impacted by violence and trauma are illustrated below: clergy retreats and facilitated reflection groups.

Clergy Retreats

In the early stages of the disillusionment phase, questions abound and gathering clergy together for a retreat is an excellent way to provide care and support for those who have been caring for and supporting their congregations and communities. Such retreats are typically all-day events held at a nice retreat center (or other suitable location) at least several miles from the impacted community—a place where clergy can gather with a sense of being away from the everyday demands of ministry. The goals of the clergy retreats are to help the clergy locate themselves in the four phases of response (see chart 2 in the introduction); to provide some space for spiritual reflection; to share stories; to provide an opportunity for community to form; to help the clergy realize they are not "alone in this"; to affirm how hard this work is and what a good job the clergy are doing in addressing the needs of their particular congregations; to worship together and to bless the clergy and their ongoing work; and to say "thank you" on behalf of God, the church universal, the community, the congregation, the people impacted or lost in the event—just a simple, heartfelt "thank you."

> *Responders were invited to conduct clergy care retreats in the aftermath of both the shootings in Tucson and Newtown. As a basis for these retreats, the four movements of Psalm 23 were chosen. But rather than begin with the first movement of "stillness and restoration," the retreat began with verse 4—walking through the valley of the shadow of death. The agenda for the day was built around working through these four movements: (1) an unexpected walk through the valley of death, (2) the comfort of a companion and the unexpected blessings one has experienced in the past months since the event, (3) leaving a wake of goodness and mercy as one's confidence in the future is restored, and finally, (4) the need and invitation to self-care—stillness, restoration of one's soul, discerning the right path for moving ahead. The richness of these retreats is the way the Spirit of God moves in and does the ministry that is necessary at the time: tears are shed, past hurts are revealed, anger bubbles over, friendships form, renewal begins, or at the very least, people simply begin to breathe a little deeper again.*

Helping the clergy of a community locate themselves in the ongoing response, reflect upon the overwhelming demands of the ministry in the recent past, share their stories, begin to create meaning out of the senseless, and affirm their ministry going forward are important elements of a clergy retreat.

Facilitated Reflection Groups

Along the same lines as the clergy retreat above, facilitated reflection groups are good for any group (staff of church, youth group, choir) highly impacted by a human-caused disaster. This is particularly true if the victims or survivors of an event, or their spouses, partners, parents, or children are members of the group. The ideal way to offer this sort of group support is to have an outsider (a counselor, clergy from another area, a professor, or volunteer) with specialization in processing trauma and leading retreats provide leadership for the event. The nature of these retreats will be highly subject to the nature, proximity, and impact of the violent event. The goal of facilitated reflection groups is to create a safe space for people to learn that their responses are normal, to share their stories, to explore meanings and insights that are emerging, to allow the hurt to continue to come out, and to be affirmed in their journey. These groups are best held off-site so that people can self-select their participation. (It is important for someone to note who does not show up and gently follow up with those people.)

One reflection group was built around the interaction of Jesus and the disciples in John 21. It began, after introductions and prayers, by a suggestion to participants that Jesus was watching them struggle all night to "catch nothing." While this angered some, as they wanted immediate guidance and assistance, others were comforted by the idea that even when they didn't know it, they were still in relationship with the Lord. They were being watched (and cared for) by God from a distance, for a time, while doing what they thought was best. The next move of the retreat was to hear the invitation to "try something new, to fish on the other side of the boat." Participants spent a lot of time thinking about "the other side" of the tragedy, where abundance and reward for their efforts resided. The group then broke for lunch, but in the context of the invitation of Jesus to "bring some of what you caught to the fire." Members of the group were invited to take their insights and reflections and think through how they might comingle with the affirmations Jesus offers in the Gospel of John, and feed their own souls and nourish their own faith. After lunch, participants came back together through a communion-type service, where each wrote down one thing he or she had learned to be thankful about since the event, and there was a sort of communion service for the soul where each came forward and picked out a slip of paper and offered it to the community on behalf of the common good. The day closed with a ritualized liturgy of affirmation and love. A song was sung as each went forward to the three leaders who were standing in a line across the front of the space. Each leader asked, "Do you love me?"; and when the person responded, "Yes, you know that I do," they were told to continue "feeding the sheep" and "tending the lambs." The last person, however, startled everyone by not saying, "Feed my sheep," as expected. Instead, she simply held the person's hands and said, "You too are loved and cared for. Do not forget this love." It was a beautiful day in the midst of an ugly season of life.

Providing dedicated time away as a group, having an outside facilitator, and being able to work together at creating meaning and discovering significance during the disillusionment phase is important work to accomplish. In the midst of what is often the bleakest period of a human-caused disaster response, providing impacted groups the opportunities to be together in appropriate and intentional ways to work through some of what they are thinking, feeling, seeing, and perceiving is one way to encourage stability and resilience in their ministry or service to the community.

CLERGY SELF-CARE: STRATEGIES FOR RESILIENCE

The safety service announcements prior to an airplane's departure always include this admonition, "Put on your own oxygen mask first before helping others." The unstated point is quite clear: those who don't put on their masks first will pass out and assist neither themselves nor the others they intended to assist in the first place. And worse, they will become one more person who needs assistance. So those who neglect self-care during and after a traumatic event go from being a well-intended helper to an unconscious victim of depressurization rather quickly. Self-care is about putting on one's own oxygen mask *first.*

People of faith often blanch at this idea: Tend thyself first! With whispers of Jesus laying down his life for others and laying aside the glory of heaven in order to become fully human forming our theology of ministry, clergy and lay leaders "press on toward the goal that lies before us." What they don't realize is that what lies before those who do not practice good self-care are burnout, divorce, alienated children, getting fired, leaving the ministry, and any number of other unpleasant consequences. Self-care is not self-indulgence; it is being intentional about nurturing and sustaining all of who you are and what you are called to be and do in the world. For the pastoral leader who would sustain a healthy ministry practice and support the recovery of a community following human-caused disaster, self-care is not an option. And the best way to continue (or begin) practicing self-care is to form an intentional self-care plan.

How to Create a Self-Care Plan

It may not be easy to formulate a self-care plan due to the fatigue and seemingly overwhelming demands pastors face, especially in the aftermath of trauma. Pastors and other congregational leaders should schedule a morning or afternoon some place away and take along paper and pen. One of the best ways to create a self-care plan is to sit down and do an inventory. Make lists around these questions:

— What do I love to do?
— Where are places I love to go for restoration?
— Who are my most supportive people (completely unaffiliated with the event)?
— What resources do I currently have in place for rest and resilience?
— What are some practices that I need to implement?

These categories will help leaders identify the resources they have and the resources they need to locate in order to provide the kind of care necessary to support resilient leadership. Some of the basic elements many people include in forming their self-care plan are a supportive primary physician, a counselor, a spiritual director, an exercise partner or trainer, a colleague or support group, a sabbatical, intentional family time with electronic devices off, a list of retreat centers nearby, an expanded list of places to practice a recreational activity or hobby, places of grace (coffee shop, art museum, music venue, the mall two towns over), and maybe a list of books. Resources should include those intentionally geared at feeding one's soul and those that are geared toward providing a complete and total diversion. Once a list of resources has been created, lay it aside for a day or two.

In another session, come back to the list and figure out what things can be done on a daily, weekly, monthly, quarterly, and semi-annual basis. Don't worry about when to do the things, just determine how often they can reasonably be incorporated in a routine. Be realistic. Once this is done, lay aside the list for another day or two.

Now, come back to the list and prioritize: What do you really love doing? What gives you life? What do you know is good for you even though you may not yet do it regularly or at all? Once this prioritization is done, formulate the plan. Some plans are built around time sections: every day I will try to . . . ; in the next week or two I will . . . ; every month I will . . . ; once a quarter I will. . . . Other plans are built around different areas of life that need attention: emotional, spiritual, physical, familial, vocational, or relational. Use whatever categories make the most sense. The point is to work the process of identifying resources and writing out the plan, and then follow it. Self-care is not an elective luxury; it is core to the healthy practice of ministry, especially in the aftermath of trauma.

> *My self-care plan may seem odd to others. As a pastor who is a total introvert, my plan is all centered on being alone and doing what I need to do to be okay with my God, myself, my family, the church I serve, and the community I'm a part of. Since the first day of my ordained ministry I've had a spiritual director. What I didn't have was a primary-care physician, a therapist, or a mentor. After the incident in the community I serve, I realized that most pastors leave the congregations they serve at some point in the first year or two after a violent traumatic event. I didn't want to be someone who needed to leave in order to be okay.*
>
> *I knew I needed to do two things: find people/professionals who could help me with my emotional, spiritual, and physical well-being; and get out of town as often as I could while still keeping my job. Thanks to a wonderful spiritual director, I was informed that fly-fishing was a spiritual discipline of the highest magnitude. Thus, on my calendar, "prayer retreat" equals time standing in a stream waiting for a trout to enjoy a barbless fly. In the immediate aftermath of the event, probably about a month or so afterward, the church paid for my family to get away for a long weekend at a retreat. This was an important part of my self-care plan—to be able to share my grief and the grief of my family away from the everyday demands of my church. I also realized, at one point, that our recycle bin was filled with a lot of (too many) empty wine bottles. I was coming home and numbing out. I brought this insight to my therapist and spiritual director, both of whom invited me to be attentive to the feelings and emotions underneath and to think about ways to transition from work to home that are healthier for me. I think the key to a good self-care plan is make the plan, implement the plan, be attentive, and, if it's not working, shred the plan and start over. In the six years since the event in my community, I've probably had ten plans; they keep changing. What doesn't change is my awareness that I need to take care of myself first. It took a while to realize I was not being selfish, I was being faithful to all that God is calling me to be and do.*

Make a plan. Follow the plan. Discern what parts of the plan are working; keep them. Discern what parts of the plan are not working; dump them. Schedule regular visits with support people. Do whatever is necessary to nurture and sustain a sense of well-being in life and in ministry. A self-care plan is a road map to ongoing wellness. And one final, personal word to those who care for others in the wake of trauma: be kind to yourself. You are tired. Life looks a little less colorful. Regular, routine items take a bit more effort. Be gracious to yourself as you form and implement your self-care plan.

The next chapter addresses considerations for worship and theological reflection during the season of disillusionment.

5

Worship and Wondering in the Wilderness

I used to be a search and rescue diver. In our training, we always used the buddy system. There was someone to dive, and someone to back him up. When the other guy is diving, you wait . . . and then, if he gets into trouble, you go down to help him out. The trick is to follow the hose, all the way down to where the other person is . . . sometimes, all the way to the bottom. But the hardest thing is to follow the hose down to the bottom, and then see it disappear below, into the silt and the darkness and the muck and slime beneath, and know that is where you have to go. You ask yourself, "Can I take the plunge? Am I brave enough to enter the darkness to find the other?"

In the season of disillusionment following the devastation of a violent event, this is the work, and the question pastors and worship leaders must continue to ask themselves: "Am I brave enough to enter the darkness to find the Other?" The early days of disbelief, of impact, of heroism are done. The candles at the memorial have been taken away; the media have folded their tents and turned their attention elsewhere. Everything looks like it did before, but nothing is the same. Can we take the plunge? Can we follow the hose all the way down to the bottom, and then go below, to a spiritual place we have never been before? The liturgical work *below* is to be an authentic presence, bearing witness to the spiritual and emotional cost of violence. There, sacred space will be created where people can ask impossible questions, express their anger and dismay, bear the silence of God, and explore the landscape of disillusionment together.

It is vitally important for those who design and lead worship in this season to practice good self-care, and to make intentional time to reflect upon and be present to the unfolding impact of the event on themselves as well as upon their congregation and community. The preacher and liturgist are continuing to follow that hose down, beneath the muck and slime and into places they can neither see nor imagine. For this work, the preacher, like a diver, needs a relaxed body, a direction, and an anchor. If one understands the liturgical structure of the worship service as the hose, the shape of the liturgy anchors the liturgist and worship leader to safety, and, at the same time, guides them into the unknown below. As a worshiping congregation moves through disillusionment, the hose, that is, the structure of worship, may remain the same, but the worshiping community is all the time going more deeply into the meaning and the power of the event that has changed their lives. Therefore, the surrounding landscape will change, the nature of the life seen at each successive level will vary, and what is noticed will be different. How those insights and observations are brought into sacred speech is the art of unfolding worship during the season of disillusionment.

We have a lady in the church, a widow thirty years old, with two children. She doesn't work, she doesn't have a degree, her father is dead. Her husband was killed by a sniper. Her question to me is this: "Why has God abandoned me?"

What can I say? How am I to preach in the face of such questions? I have been studying the scriptures to find a word that will help my people in these times, and I have seen two things. First, I need now to stay away from the old wisdom texts that say bad things happen because you are a sinner. Instead, I am discovering again apocalyptic literature. They were living in crisis because they were faithful. What is happening to us is not because of sin. God will one day interfere and that day is near and this hard situation will end and the believer should stand fast, be patient, and preserve their values.

WEEKLY WORSHIP

In the immediate wake of a traumatic event, the suggested framework for worship is *letting go, letting be, letting begin.* During this longer season of disillusionment, framing worship around these rubrics will help the pastor and worship team find rich language to support the congregation as it moves along the path through the valley of the shadow, and dares to explore the spiritual landscape of disillusionment. Another way to shape the flow of Sunday worship in this season is to imagine the movements as *Relenting, Revealing,* and *Remembering.*

Relenting

As a congregation moves through disillusionment, and the adrenaline of the heroic phase drains away, leaders and people will enter into a season of letdown, which opens up the space into which anger, loss, and depression begin to emerge. It is like that parable of Jesus, about the man who swept his house clean of an evil spirit and put nothing in its place (Matt. 12:43–45). Because the house was left empty, said Jesus, seven additional evil spirits came to abide, more powerful than the first. Though it may seem dangerous to leave the worship house empty by not restoring a sense of normalcy as quickly as possible, the "empty house" is a necessary feature of the season of disillusionment. The ability to tolerate and even welcome negative expressions and feelings is vital, and the work of lament and grief that needs to happen is a part of prayer. Martin Buber, the post-Holocaust philosopher and writer, relates this story:

> One of the followers of the Rabbi of Kobryn was very poor. He complained to the rabbi about his straits, which, as he said, put him off his studies and made him unable to pray. The rabbi told him: "in these times, the greatest piety, which supersedes study and prayer, is to accept the world as it is."[1]

Entering worship week by week can be viewed as a relenting, a letting go, because in disillusionment believers are relinquishing the wishful hope that life and faith could be as they were before. Give up for the time being an insistence that the world should be otherwise, and lead the worshiping community to accept the world as it is. The opening movements of worship such as the call to worship, invocation, and prayer of confession are liturgically strong elements through which the congregation will be able to engage this movement of relenting.

The *Call to Worship* reminds the faith community that its "reasonable service"—its worship-work in this time and place—is to address both its praise and lament to God, entering the holy ground of corporate worship with openness and trust, even in difficult times. A healthy worshiping community in this season will practice a willingness to be attentive to the unfamiliar spiritual landscape of disillusionment, and to pray and wonder their way through it together. *Invocation* does not so much ask that God would show up in the valley of the shadow, but rather acknowledges that becoming present to God who is already in our midst is, during this time of dislocation, an act of intentionality for the believer: "Even though I walk through the darkest valley, I fear no evil; for you are with me" (Ps. 23:4). The church in disillusionment chooses to show up and continue together the work of walking through the dark valley. *Confession* invites the community and its leaders to accept and live into a season of lament, as they admit both a longing for answers and the impossibility of finding them. Following a terrorist attack in his community, one pastor put it this way:

> *Let us confess, all of us, there are many things we cannot answer. Why do human beings accept that there are natural things we do not know . . . but in spiritual things we feel we have to know? We have a measure for heat and cold . . . for darkness and light. . . . We don't ask about the answer for why or how we can measure light and darkness . . . but for some reason we feel we must be able to answer for or explain good and evil, something for which there is no answer.*

As time passes, and circumstances surrounding the story of the human-caused disaster continue to emerge, the landscape of the valley changes. What will be ritually acknowledged and released through corporate worship will, similarly, continue evolving. Pay special attention to newly emerging circumstances in news about the traumatic event, such as the (delayed) death of a victim; the arrest or arraignment, trial, or sentencing of the perpetrator; or particular marker dates, like the first month *after*. One of the most powerful examples of a pastor utilizing the unfolding story of the tragedy as a way to frame worship is described in the following story:

> *Nearly nine months after the first accusations of rape were voiced, the sheriff's office was notified, and after investigation, the youth director pled guilty to all charges brought against him. The congregation was in shock. The young man they had raised, whom so many trusted, pleading guilty to all charges of assault, rape, possession, and distribution of drugs? How could this be? He was beloved. Bewilderment, shame, anger, and a deep sense of betrayal flooded the congregation and the small-town community. After seeking advice from a consultant, from staff members, and from the governing body of the church, the pastor discerned it was time for the congregation to lament together.*
>
> *The church had never before held a service of lament. Before the service began the pastor welcomed all who had gathered. He praised them for having the courage to try a new thing and to bring their sorrow before the Lord. He read a definition of lament, and then explained that the service would have components of Scripture, each representing passages in the Bible that address lament. While the service referred to God's enduring companionship in all times and the hope that comes with Jesus Christ's presence, it did not speak of new life. That assurance*

*would come later. It was time to bring the sorrows of the congregation
and express them in the sanctuary before God.*

*Preparing for this service, the pastor struggled with what to do following
a brief welcome and description. How should the liturgy officially start? He
finally decided to begin by reading aloud the reason for their gathering, the
reason for their need to lament right now. He read as the call to worship the
official charges, according to the sheriff's office publication, finishing with
the words: This is why we are here today. Let us worship God.*

Naming a community's passage through the valley of the shadow
invites the prayer-speech of anger, grief, and lament. It nourishes the
fragile beginnings of a new conversation, rooted in utter honesty and
naked in need. This is a conversation whose ending cannot be imagined, but without which faith cannot hope to survive or thrive. It is
our conversation, our chance, and our responsibility: no one else's.
One of the great ancient Hasidic masters, Rabbi Barukh of Med-
zebozh, put it this way: "I know there are questions that have no
answers; there is a suffering that has no name; there is injustice in
God's creation;—and there are reasons enough for man to explode
with rage. I know there are reasons for you to be angry. Good. Let us
be angry. Together."[2]

Revealing

The second movement of worship, in which the community listens for
a word from God as Scripture is read and the Word proclaimed, might
in this season become a moment for thoughtful and tender exploration
of the landscape of disillusionment. It is a time for walking the *via
negativa*, uncovering that which we do not understand and cannot ever
know about God. This theological work is vitally important, but may
seem dangerous to some. Following the violence of September 11, one
pastor actually described his experience of disillusionment as a work
of apocalypse, uncovering. In November 2001, pastors from the New
York City area participated in a series of retreats with colleagues and
national responders. They were gathering for reflection and spiritual
support while finding their way through the "strange land" of crisis
and disillusionment and trying to lead their congregations through the
valley of the shadow. Several months later, the pastor shared how his
experience in those days seemed like struggling with recovery from an
illness. He talked about how the root of the word *recovery* means "to

cover up again," and how much that re-covering felt like a denial of the cost of injury in his life. He said he yearned for a different word to speak about healing than *recovery*. In a powerful reflection, written for the first anniversary of September 11, he described it this way:

> While my illness pales in comparison to the cataclysm of September 11, it was an introduction to powerlessness. After September 11, for months, vivid nightmares would come to me, replaying the events' endless video loop. Those visitations have now ceased, and I don't want to see those scenes over again, but neither do I want to cover it all up. I want to remember and reflect. I don't want to compound all the losses by forgetting. I want to know something of the truth, something more than I had known on September 10. I long for understanding, yet I feel like some cloud, some shadow of confusion, has settled over my psyche. My previous ways of making sense of the world, my faith, and my nation no longer fit. . . . In John, Jesus says, "You will know the truth, and the truth will make you free." The word used for truth is *alethia*, or "not forgetting." Perhaps remembering is key to knowing truth as well as an antidote to confusion.[3]

He went on to describe how he engaged in a search of biblical Greek to find a word for *recovery*, which in the original language of the New Testament does not exist. Instead, he found the Greek word for *cover*, *kalypto*, the opposite of which is *apokalypto*, to uncover or unveil. His conclusion:

> First, truth is more to be found in uncovering than recovering. Second, pop culture uses the word *apocalypse* to mean "The End." An apocalyptic event—as horrible as it is—may not be "The End." It may be the beginning of a new understanding. I am not willing to surrender the events of September 11 to senselessness or hopelessness or despair. I want to look into the abyss and see what it holds. I tenaciously hang on to the conviction that meaning exists in this and that new depths of meaning will emerge through all the disorientation. Sometimes the abyss reveals what cannot be known otherwise—about the world and about God. One of my seminary professors, James Loder, taught that the void is the prelude to the holy. The awful can be awe-filled.[4]

As texts are chosen and sermons developed through this season, the preacher might ask: What is being uncovered as this hard story continues to unfold? What do we notice? What do we feel? In the phase of disillusionment, there is no intent to force any conclusions or particular shape on the faith experience. The mode is, rather, permissive and inquiring. This is a way of wandering in the wilderness. The faith community is accepting a season of thirst and hunger, receiving with gratitude the rare gifts of sustenance in the desert, and clinging to one another as they try to find a way out of the valley of the shadow into the homeland that has been promised. "God is at home," said Meister Eckhart, the medieval German mystic, "we are in the far country."[5]

There are many powerful examples in sacred text of our ancestors in faith engaging this difficult walk through the far country of disillusionment with courage, trust, and grace. "A wandering Aramean was my ancestor," begins one such affirmation in the Torah of Moses, "and he went down into Egypt and lived there as an alien, few in number" (Deut. 26:5). The stories of Adam and Eve's exile from Eden, the banishment of Hagar and Ishmael, the lonely journeys of Jacob, and the trials of his son Joseph are rich narratives through which a congregation's experience after human-caused disaster may be explored. So, too, the psalms of lament, the book of Job, the prophetic narratives of the exile in Isaiah, Jeremiah, Jonah, and Lamentations, and the Gospel narratives that describe Jesus' journey through temptation, suffering, and death. Where is the community in the unfolding story of its own passion narrative? What is being revealed by imaginatively entering that passion story in worship? As the community moves through this phase, some weeks will be deeper, more somber than others. A balance of lament, compassionate comfort, and emergent hope will shape a pastoral approach to preaching during this time.

Remembering, or Re-membering

Reflecting on the road to Emmaus text in Luke 24:13–35, Fred Craddock observes:

> There are three times in which to know an event: in rehearsal, at the time of the event, and in remembrance. In rehearsal, understanding is hindered by an inability to believe that the event will really occur or that it will be so important. At the time of the event, understanding is hindered by the clutter and confusion of so much so fast. But in remembrance, the nonseriousness of rehearsal and the busyness of the event give way to recognition, realization, and understanding.[6]

The final movement of worship, which shifts the community toward engagement and return to the world outside of the sanctuary, customarily includes pastoral prayers, prayers of the people, offerings, hymns, charges, and benedictions or blessings. This part of the service is always transitional, helping move the people, following their encounter with God and with sacred text, back into their everyday lives. During the season of disillusionment, this transition is more important than ever, as it helps build a bridge from moments of refuge and sanctuary back into the dissonant realities of life after public violence. Craddock's observations about remembrance as a way of finding recognition and understanding are helpful here. In the Emmaus story from Luke 24, two disciples, after meeting Jesus on the road and breaking bread with him, recognized the Lord, remembered what Christ had taught, found a renewed sense of peace and purpose in the midst of loss, and returned with joy to tell the story to their friends. Their experience of listening, breaking bread, and being present to God helped them remember their faith story, and be re-membered to one another: that is, to return from the isolation of sorrow and disillusionment into community. In the season of disillusionment, bread for the journey is important, both as the church celebrates the Eucharist and in the breaking of bread during fellowship meals. The many years of "practice" at the Table—reciting the story of the Lord's betrayal, suffering, and death while sharing a meal in community—become poignantly real after public violence and trauma. As leaders and members grapple with the effects of human-caused disaster, the betrayals, abandonments, suffering and death, practice, and recitation become reality; and the church is still, nevertheless, at Table together.

Let the closing movements of worship send the people back into the world, and trust that the experience in worship is re-membering them to the Source of their hope, renewing their connection with one another and with the larger community as they continue the journey in the wilderness.

RITUAL AND SACRAMENT

Memorials

For many congregations, supplementary opportunities to gather for prayer, reflection, and fellowship are welcomed at this time, especially in the first month or two following a human-caused disaster. Some communities build and tend spontaneous memorials, with candles, pictures, flowers, or the like. There is a kind of natural cycle to the usefulness of such memorial sites, and when it becomes evident that the memorial has served its purpose, consider gathering a few people who found meaning in its presence to help ritually and prayerfully dismantle it. The January 2011 shooting in Tucson, Arizona, which killed seven and wounded Congresswoman Gabrielle Giffords, took place in a supermarket parking lot that was roped off with yellow police tape for many days. During those days, a spontaneous memorial was created by neighbors and residents who brought flowers, signs, and candles to honor the community's tragic losses. An interfaith group of faith leaders decided to visit the site when the tape and memorial were to be removed. Together, dressed in each tradition's formal liturgical robes, the clergy used incense, prayers, and music to "sanctify" the space where the violence happened, and then return that space to everyday human use. Neighbors who had gathered there were provided with a powerful ritual opportunity to move forward together and demonstrate respect for what had happened, while at the same time restoring their neighborhood shopping center to its ordinary purposes.

Special Services

Prayer services using the traditions of the communities of Taizé or Iona[7] can provide comfort, support, and space for reflection for a congregation or community in lament. Services with minimal exposition that are simple in design and provide generous space for stillness, prayer, Scripture, and comforting music are accessible to many different kinds of congregations and helpful to many people.

According to the comfort, style, and traditions of the congregation, rituals such as a service of anointing for wholeness, a baptismal renewal, or a prayerful labyrinth walk may be combined, integrated into Sunday worship, or offered on their own for families, children, and youth as well as the general congregation as ways to comfort and sustain people during the phase of disillusionment.

The Liturgical Calendar

In the small congregation whose story has been related previously, returning to the sanctuary after the shooting death of their organist on the first

Sunday of Advent seemed unbearable. After the crime scene tape was removed, a small memorial with candles grew on the outside steps, and each night the warm light shined into the vacant sanctuary. The congregation met for worship with the neighboring Lutherans, and decided they could not contemplate returning to their sanctuary until sometime after Christmas. But when, and how? In conversation with the pastor, a simple, eloquent plan began to unfold. Epiphany, the liturgical end of the Christmas season, is the sixth of January. That year, it occurred on a Saturday. On Epiphany, the day of the Bethlehem star's appearing, the journey of the magi, and the beginning of the season of light, members of the choir and congregation gathered on the steps of the church, took down the candle memorial and the unused Christmas decorations, and prepared the sanctuary for worship. A simple, unstructured service of blessing and renewal re-consecrated their violated worship space. Members of most of the neighboring congregations in the town sent representatives to attend, showing the still-traumatized congregation that they were not alone, and brought casseroles and desserts for a shared meal following the service. Soon after the doors opened that morning, the small sanctuary was full: of people, of memory, of a sense of connection and community that powerfully bridged the difficult transition back into the congregation's sacred space. It was the beginning of a journey toward Wisdom.

Though not every congregation follows the lectionary and the formal seasons of the church year, the appointed readings for each Sunday that frame the Christian story—through both Testaments and the Psalms—can be a rich resource to connect the spirituality of disillusionment with the story of salvation. On the Sunday following September 11, 2001, many pastors were stunned to find that the appointed psalm for that Sunday in the Revised Common Lectionary was Psalm 74, a deep lament over the destruction of Jerusalem that vividly described the community's despair and sense of abandonment by God as the smoke from the rubble of the temple rose over the ruined city. The words framed by the church's ancestors in faith were eerily evocative of the daily images everyone had seen of the smoking ruins of the Twin Towers.

During particular seasons of the church year, services framed around the liturgical calendar may be especially resonant for congregations in lament: the seasons of Advent and Lent, with their balance of reflection, confession, and anticipation are strong themes for the phase of disillusionment. Ash Wednesday reminds believers of the frailty of human life; Maundy Thursday, Good Friday, and Passion Sunday services speak strongly to the experience of public violence. More contemporary expressions in the church calendar, like the "Longest Night" or "Blue Sunday" services many congregations now use for members who are in a season of grieving during the Christmas season, can be easily adapted and are richly rewarding expressions of worship as well.

Sacrament

Ritual enactments and liturgies that are central to church tradition, like baptism and the Lord's Supper, connect participants spiritually and emotionally to a source of comfort, continuity, and meaning-making. These liturgies are common practice in the life of the church, and in addition, they connect to sound healing practices. Trauma theory supports this understanding that ritual can reframe and support the healing task:

> Trauma theory has something to say with regard to the repetitive ritual action we call the liturgy. . . .
> The source of ritual remembering is a sharing of bread and wine. It is not the violence of the cross. Ritual, in this document, breaks the spiral of violence, notably, the spiral of religious violence—sacrifice. . . .
> The cross has come to symbolize the gospel for us, but what are Jesus' instructions? "Do this in remembrance of me . . ." Jesus points not to the cross but to the meal as the place of remembering. The sharing of bread and wine—not the violent death—becomes a form of ritual remembering that disrupts violence.[8]

The Cross-Place: An Invitation

To understand the transforming power of worship during the phase of disillusionment, we conclude with a story from early in the Gospel of Mark. Jesus was off by himself praying, and his disciples were searching for him. "When they found him, they said to him, 'Everyone is searching for you.' He answered, 'Let us go on to the neighboring towns, so that I may proclaim the message there also; for that is what I came out to do'" (Mark 1:37–38). But as they set out to do their mission, a leper stopped them in the road, asking Jesus to choose to do something else, instead—to be present to his suffering and to heal him. The story tells us that Jesus, moved with pity, stretched out his hand and healed the man—an action that both distracted and delayed Jesus from the work he believed he was called to do, and also contaminated Jesus, since it was believed that to touch a leper was to become unclean, infected with disease. Mark tells us that because Jesus chose to do this, his ministry had to change. He could no longer go into the towns openly to proclaim the message as he had planned; he was contaminated by his encounter with the suffering leper, and he had to stay outside, in the country, and wait for people to come to him. The choices we make when confronted by difficult necessity determine the direction that ministry and congregational life will take after violence or trauma. The moment of choosing is, in a very real sense, a cross-place.

In the Celtic faith tradition, the cross is a central Christian symbol, and a powerful metaphor for the human spiritual journey. It evokes gatherings, possible pathways, choices. The cross is the place where things change, the place where things fall away. The cross is a powerful image for understanding the nature of caregiving among congregations who are suffering the aftermath of public violence; for the impact of a human-caused disaster on a community is like a crucifixion. Following this metaphor, the process of disillusionment that follows the season of devastation and heroism could be described as a season of Lent—a steep slide into long, somber days of diminishment, scarcity, and darkness. Though these days may be punctuated, as Lent is, by "little Easters"—moments of gratitude for the goodness of the ordinary, and deep, unexpected experiences of joy and clarity and purposefulness—this time in a congregation's life is a complex and challenging one, marked by a certain dullness and seemingly endless wandering through the wilderness of grief, bewilderment, and loss. No one would choose it; most will still prefer to avoid it. But there is no Easter without Good Friday; and Lent, however painful a season, is the way Jesus and the church walked through the valley of the shadow that concluded with death and resurrection.

The intersection of ministry and public violence is a cross-place: a moment and circumstance in which pastors and the communities of faith they serve must choose what path they will walk, because they cannot go back to the place they were before. Worship in the months that follow events like these are, in a way, a continuing series of cross-places. In the story from the Gospel of Mark, Jesus chose one path when he was confronted by suffering, and thereafter he could not go back to the ministry he had planned before. Violence in church or community demands such choices from us. When we, like Jesus, choose to stop, touch, and be contaminated by the impact of human-caused disaster, it changes our ministry, our preaching, and our worship. No longer can we stay safely inside the villages. We have to work outside, in the far country, where the people who need us can find us. To craft worship outside our safe liturgical village is a risk we are invited to take, a powerful and demanding experience, and a place where astonishing transformation can occur in the life of a people of faith.

In the next chapter, the hard, dark work of disillusionment begins to turn upward toward the light in the phase of Reforming, which shapes the healing journey toward wisdom.

6

Phase Three: Reforming toward Wisdom

During a reflection on Psalm 137 at the pastoral consultation in the Middle East, which story is related above, the powerful truths voiced by our ancestors in faith came alive as participants described their own deep sense of sadness; their feelings of helplessness, loss, and grief. The incalculable human cost of violence and trauma in the lives of individuals and communities was tangible in the room; no longer merely ancient words on a page. Near the close of the session, the wife of a pastor from Iraq spoke. Their congregation had been sheltering sixty displaced families for over a year. They overcame great fear in order to welcome those refugees, and in addition were supporting and visiting families in a refugee camp an hour away. She saw something different in the psalm: hope. She slowly repeated a verse from the psalm, "On the willows there they hung up their harps." Awe and gratitude filled her voice as she continued, "They didn't destroy their harps. They could have cast them down, and broken them to pieces, but instead, they hung them up. This shows us that they hoped for a better future. They believed they would have a future. Though now was not the time for singing, someday, there would be singing again."

In the journey of individuals and congregations beyond the landscape of trauma, there comes a decisive moment of turning. This turning may seem subtle, and yet it is strong. Its character is shaped by the settling of disillusionment into acceptance, the resolution of grief, and the easing of lament into a direction of hope. Herein lies the foundation for the good work of *Reforming*.

Substantive reforming cannot begin until a congregation has encountered an "and yet" moment. This moment is signified on the chart in the introduction as the turning point upward from the pit of disillusionment (see p. xiv). The "and yet" moment derives from Lamentations 3 in the Bible. In the first two chapters of heart-wrenching exhortation, the author of Lamentations bears painful witness before God of all that has gone on in the violent destruction of Jerusalem. Yet in chapter 3, the author expresses two truths: this catastrophe has happened, *and yet*, God abides (see Lam. 3:20–22). When present-day people of faith experience this profound realization in their personal journeys or as a community along its trajectory of healing, a turning point is reached. The ability to begin building anew is engendered from an internal strength that is neither pretense nor equivocation. There is no formula for forecasting precisely when this turn occurs among a congregation; and this phase, like the others, can be uneven in its progress. It may contain intermittent confusion and is often infused with conflict. It requires intentional commitment to stay together and work together to build up one other and the beloved community again. It is a re-visioning and a rebuilding of purpose and priorities.

On Sunday, December 16, 2012, congregations around the country faced a significant challenge. The liturgical calendar was at the Third Sunday of Advent, on which date most were scheduled to light the rose-colored candle that for many congregations signifies joy. This was especially challenging in Newtown, Connecticut, where two days earlier, a young man had entered Sandy Hook Elementary School and shot and killed twenty children and six adults. How could any church speak of *joy* on that Sunday? At the Newtown Congregational Church, the pastoral staff wrestled with this quandary and decided to proceed with the liturgy as planned. At that service and in each of the vigils of that weekend, they also acknowledged their heartache through many forms of expression. The pastor explained their decision this way, "Joy is not the same as happiness. Happiness is fleeting, it comes and goes. Joy is a gift from God. We light the candle of Joy to remind ourselves, in any season of life that we are in, of this gift and that joy is not determined or manufactured by our circumstances."[1]

Other congregations and pastors in Connecticut and around the country made different choices. The following year, as another congregation lived through their own season of disillusionment, they decided to switch the Advent candles permanently. Joy, for them, now falls on a different Sunday than it did traditionally. Their pastor explained the decision this way, "At some point in history, a group of people created the Advent wreath and candle-lighting tradition and decided the order. That worked for them in their circumstances. Now, today, with our circumstances, it is more meaningful to us to do it differently. We are still a part of this ancient tradition, but are practicing it in a way that speaks our story as well."[2] Pastors, especially in the phase of Reforming, will have many opportunities to explore and discern what practices of worship and mission create hindrances and what practices promote faithfulness best, given the character and identity of their congregations.

During this phase, as the congregation and community move forward, they also will experience periodic marker events that slow or temporarily pause progress. These may be anniversaries, birthdays, or other obvious reminders of what used to be before the violence and loss of life. Marker events also may not be so obvious. Proms, graduations, a gathering at a favorite restaurant, a certain song on the radio, or a certain commute, can all evoke poignant reminders, momentarily stealing one's breath away. Reforming involves learning how to create new habits and traditions in meaningful ways. This can be a challenge especially during the first two years following trauma, a time full of emotion when members of the congregation are often in different places on the spectrums of grief and healing. But gradually, as the months and years pass, new forms and practices emerge in ways that honor the integrity of what has passed and at the same time welcome the glimmers of new life ahead.

PASTORAL LEADERSHIP

Just as the pastor's shift from the heroic phase toward disillusionment supports the shift of the congregation, a pastor's encounter of the "and yet" moment plays a key role in shaping the staff and congregation's experience during the phase of reforming.

Just outside the perimeter of a large city, a community experienced a shooting at a local football game. The field was across the street from a prominent church. The incident left one youth group member in critical condition, and other community members injured or in shock. Several weeks after the girl returned home from the hospital, I called the youth pastor to see how those affected by the event were doing. In the course of our conversation, he said, "This was tragic and horrible. It was deeply painful for so many of us. At the same time, and it's kind of weird to say, but we feel like we were ready to handle this. We very much feel God's presence with us. She's received good medical care, and we have some good counselors we know and trust for her, her family, and some of her friends in the youth group. We felt like the gatherings we hosted for the youth, for parents, and for the congregation were received well and were meaningful. We feel like we are in a place to walk with her and her family, as we all heal."

It can be a sign of denial or resistance to the impact of trauma when pastoral leaders say, "We're fine. We did everything right." Sometimes, though, it is the case that the pastor and the congregation are prepared and able to respond well. In the midst of heartache and the overwhelming impact of violence, many pastoral leaders are managing well and drawing on resources that, for them, represent best practices.

Worth considering here is what causes the "and yet" moment for the pastor? What varying components enable a pastor to become attuned to a sense of God's abiding and faithful presence even when faced with tragic destruction? For some, a gentle, intuitive awareness may awaken in them that *now* is the time. For others, it may be that the "and yet" moment is wrung from a Jacob-like wrestling between self and a divine presence shrouded in darkness, until a new and hopeful naming releases them to welcome the light of a new day. It may be that dynamics among the congregation and leadership force a poignant encounter, causing a jolting sense of reawakening to new possibilities.

However the "and yet" moment unfolds personally for the pastor and communally for the congregation, pastors frequently encounter obstacles at this stage. For many there is a lingering sadness. Some congregation members may assert active resistance to moving forward. In this new and strenuous phase, reforming and rebuilding requires a lot of the pastor's energy as leader; the pastor may also find herself or himself resistant at times. It may be due to a lack of resources, such as money, time, leaders, or information. In rare cases, a congregation may find that they do not want to let go of their identity of being traumatized. The attention, energy, and gathering around the crises may continue to be overly attractive or be feeding other kinds of personal aches. To further frustrate matters, pastors and staff often experience conflict in this phase. As each views the congregation's process through the lens of his or her own recovery, their differing locations on the path of healing may shape strong and divergent convictions about what is best for the congregation *now*, potentially engendering conflict.

The time of reforming is slow going. There will be welcome moments of surprise and inspiration, even as it continues to feel as though the community is taking two steps forward and one step backward. It is important for pastors to trust their sense of leadership during this phase. Strong collegial support makes a difference as does consistent encouragement and modeling of appropriate self-care and a calming presence. During this phase many pastors experience a renewed sense of calling, a new name or identity (like Jacob-Israel) that, though won through struggle, points toward a rich and rewarding future. In fact, the congregation as a whole may begin to sense resolution to the trauma incident, and turn toward a deepening of missional identity. Personally, pastors begin to experience new energy, direction, and sense of purpose. They can identify and affirm gifts and new ministries among the staff and lay leaders, too. Together, the leadership and congregation begin to rediscover joy as they work through the season of reforming.

CLERGY SELF-CARE

Self-care is critically important in this season of response. The identifying characteristic of this phase of human-caused disaster response is an intentional turn toward restoration. The key to self-care at this stage, especially when compassion fatigue may have set in, is to be intentional and accountable; take time to develop a self-care plan and then follow it.

Creating a self-care plan need not be laborious or tedious. It can be fun and life-giving to simply sit back and reflect upon all the things that give life. What did you love to do before the incident? How did you take care of yourself prior to the increased demands of the human-caused disaster response? What do you need to do in order to become the person you know God wants you to be or the person you want to be? The key is to be intentional, to write the plan out, and then follow that plan for restoration and renewal with persistence.

Months after the tragedy, I was so weary and tired and ready to quit the ministry. I went away to a retreat center for two days of quiet. I took a notepad and a pen—no Bible, no book, no computer. My idea was to be in prayer, asking the question: What gives me "life" and "joy"? I had planned long hours of deep prayer and solitude. I had hoped for great insights and new perspectives. I wanted the "aha" moment. Instead, I slept—a lot! I sat outside the first morning and slept all afternoon. I went to the dining hall and had dinner by myself, off in the corner. After returning to my room, I went to bed early and slept soundly until the next morning, my final morning. As I sat drinking coffee, looking out over the landscape, the sun already shining and the hills a beautiful tapestry of browns and purples, it dawned on me: I love retreating—sitting in places like this, drinking coffee, thinking, praying, wondering about the future, and waiting for God to speak. I started to make a grocery list under the heading: things I love to do. My list included retreating, making love to my spouse, cooking dinners, fly-fishing, walking in the woods, waking early and drinking a cup of coffee as the sun rises, writing with a fountain pen, and on and on. . . . When I shared this list with my spiritual director, he laughed and said I could rename my list "embodied prayer." He encouraged me to do all the things I listed as regularly as possible and to rejoice in them.

In creating an intentional self-care plan it is often helpful to find someone to work with—a spiritual director, counselor, or another pastor—people who are attentive to the ebb and flow of the soul. It might also be helpful to have a physician, a dietician, and a personal trainer involved in creating a self-care plan. Be practical and specific. One pastor decided to include "eat three vegetarian dinners per week" as part of the self-care plan, and worked with someone who specialized in vegetarian and vegan meal planning. A self-care plan during this season is particular and even peculiar; it needs to be authentic to the individual making it. The key is intentionality and grace; follow it, understanding it may not be possible to stick to the plan completely. This is part of the fun, mapping self-care activities relative to the plan one has created. Learn what works and what does not. Be attentive to what gives life, what renews a sense of strength, purpose, and joy. At regular intervals (monthly or quarterly) take out the plan and assess how it is going. Tweak the plan moving forward and be gracious every step of the way. Pastoral self-care is about doing the important work of cultivating and nurturing one's own resilience, which allows a pastor to continue caring for and ministering with the congregation.

One common symptom among leaders and caregivers following human-caused disaster is compassion fatigue. Compassion fatigue can be described as a combination of *burnout* (a chronic perception of too many demands with too few resources to meet those needs) and *secondary (or caregiver) traumatic stress.* Secondary traumatic stress is the accumulation of trauma narratives heard and internalized by those whose work is to listen to and support trauma survivors. Many pastors, clinicians, and caregivers—who repeatedly hear and carry with them the traumatic stories of those in their charge—experience symptoms similar to those of post-traumatic stress. Therapeutic support is recommended if compassion fatigue is acute, interfering significantly with work or life. In some instances, pastors, staff members, and congregants need to participate in regular counseling in order to work through aspects of their human-caused disaster response. The demands on leaders of congregations responding to human-caused disasters are tremendous.

Finding someone to care for the caretakers is a good and necessary intervention supporting a healthy return to a place of well-being for all. Having a safe space to talk about and process the impact of caring for others in the valley of the shadow of death can be very beneficial. The key is to find a good counselor, spiritual director, or therapist, someone knowledgeable about the impact of trauma and compassion fatigue. Pastoral leaders need to do whatever it takes to restore resilience and a positive sense of purpose and mission; their health, as well as the well-being of the congregation, may rely on it.

STAFF AND LAY EXPERIENCES

It had been almost two years since the incident, and intuitively the pastor felt that something was not right among the congregation and the usually very healthy staff. He was not able to put into words what he sensed was causing a general malaise and lack of energy or inspiration. He described the congregation as "motion-making rather than meaning-making." During a three-day staff retreat and workshop, participants accomplished some very good work together. Still, the conversation was raw and direct and emotional. At one moment in the afternoon, feeling frustrated, the pastor blurted out: "What is preventing us from moving forward? What's going on?" The response was silence, which quickly turned uncomfortable. A chart was put up on the wall and members of the staff were invited to write on an index card where they each saw the team located on the graph of a disaster recovery cycle. One after the other, each one indicated that as a staff they were in the reforming phase. That was a great surprise to the pastor, who was still functioning in disillusionment. The strength of the staff pushed him into realizing that it was time for all of them to move toward reforming together.

Staff and lay leadership have an important role in the "and yet" moment of turning toward restoration and throughout the process. Depending on the persons and the culture of the congregation that existed prior to the incident of violence, staff can contribute positively or negatively. There will be conflict in this phase regardless of the health of the staff. Staff will both contribute to and be the recipients of conflict. During the phase of Reforming, staff may experience themselves as being pushed and pulled by one another and by the congregation. In this season, *direction* is more important than the *pace* at which the staff and congregation are moving. As shown on chart 2 in the introduction, expect this time to be a period of jagged growth. Just as the staff may find they need to push a pastor who is "stuck" for whatever reason, it is also critical that the staff support the leadership of the pastor. This is a delicate art during this phase. Best practices usually come about when staff members stay focused on building a healthy team wherein each person recognizes that regaining momentum is everyone's focal point.

Staff and member transitions can be expected in the phase of Reforming. As the entire group moves through the phase of Disillusionment and gains more clarity about what happened and who they are in the aftermath, people may experience their own sense of identity or calling differently and in ways that draw them away from the congregation. This can happen for a variety of reasons. Congregations may find that people are newly attracted to becoming members in the aftermath of crises, perhaps even because of observing the congregation's response to the traumatic incident. They also may find that, in the aftermath, different leadership skills are now needed that necessitate hiring someone new or obtaining professional consulting services to assist with the stages of Reforming.

Throughout these transitions, certain practices have proven to be most helpful. Staff members should celebrate moments of goodness and surprises of joy. The practice of self-care continues to be very important. Staff members also should maintain appropriate boundaries with one another and congregation members. These things assist in the resolution of the congregational trauma. Personally, staff and members of the congregation will be likely to experience new senses of energy, direction, and purpose. As they affirm one another and lay leaders' gifts and new ministries, together they will rediscover joy and stability.

CONGREGATIONAL CARE

Some have named this place where we are rooted
a place of death.
We fix them with our callous eyes
and call it, rather, a terrain of resurrection.
          —Robin Morgan, "Easter Island: I Embarkation"[3]

The Terrain of Resurrection

The anniversary, or one-year marker, of a human-caused disaster is a date on a calendar toward which people yearn and around which the media will gather, so that remembrance can be made, the distance toward recovery assessed, and the hard work of survival celebrated. An often unspoken expectation of many people is that, if the first terrible year can just pass, everything will be okay. Yet for many people impacted by a violent event, a year is not such a long time. While the world outside hopes and wishes that the afflicted community will prove its resilience by being entirely recovered at the year's end, for most people this is not so, and the expectation of full recovery places a burden on survivors that is unreasonable. Certainly a large part of the hard work of disillusionment has been undertaken, addressed, and survived. Yet even as the phase of disillusionment begins to yield its tenacious hold on the majority of the congregation, there will still be some who are left behind, stuck in anger, struggling with emptiness, seeking an old familiar companionship with God and neighbor that remain stubbornly elusive. Many of these people will not speak about what they are feeling. Others may try to keep the larger body of the community stuck back in the disillusionment in which they have become mired. A few may even have demonstrated their incapability of recovering, and may have already been referred to professional treatment, or find such referral necessary.

Pastors and congregational leaders will need to carefully assess and tend these various groups and individuals on their several paths toward healing and wholeness as they advocate for the re-formation of their community of faith in wisdom. Though a sense of return to the ordinary has not quite been achieved, there is hope that a new light is shining, and the scent of peace is in the air.

Reformed, and Always Reforming

This phase of recovery in a congregation and community's life is called *Reforming,* acknowledging historical Protestant theological roots: *reformands, et semper reformanda,* "reformed, and always reforming." When events of public violence shatter the faith community and challenge its self-understanding and theological worldview, this process-oriented affirmation is a powerful one. Circumstances beyond human control exploded reality, forcing changes in long-held assumptions about self and the ways of the world, and challenging cherished beliefs. No one sought to be challenged in this way, yet reformation became imperative because there is no going back to the way things were. There is a long and wearisome path to be trod through the valley of the shadow of death before the community of faith will find that goodness and mercy once again follow them all the days of their life. Though many may have prayed for a miracle, most will have learned that the only way out of the valley of the shadow is through it. This work is hard, necessary, and mysterious. In worship, in pastoral care, in community gathering, and in voicing the unfolding narrative of redemption from the impact of the event to the present day, those who lead the community have kept the faith. To honor the work of reformation that was thrust upon them is an important part of moving through disillusionment and into the work of reformation.

Never dismiss or minimize the cost this pastoral and congregational work demands of pastoral leaders, their families, the lay leadership of the congregation, and the people. Provide, in this season of turning, many opportunities for reflection, respite, and return. Imagine that the congregation is like Lazarus, who endured a painful illness, died, and was buried; and now, the voice of the Christ, his friend, is calling for new life: "Lazarus, come out!" (John 11:43). The pastoral leaders want to respond to this call, the church is ready to return to life and warmth and comfort, but there is still much to be tended before the tomb can be left entirely. As in the story, grave clothes are tightly wrapped about, binding body and spirit, and until they can be unwound, no one is free. The work of reforming recognizes the call to resurrection, and begins the work of unwinding so that the binding power of the grave can be broken at last.

As mentions of "the tragedy" lessen in frequency, interest in programs and participation that is not tied to the disaster begins to resurface; everything is no longer referenced as either "before" or "after," and the work of unbinding has begun. It is time to turn toward resurrection.

In congregational and pastoral life, this may be a season of small adjustments and delicate retuning. It is a time for noticing what has been laid to rest, what is still being worked out, what is beginning to be born. As members' energy returns, feel free to relinquish event-oriented programs or preoccupations—letting them go gently into memory as their purpose has been served. There might still be generous space provided for the congregation, as individuals and as a whole, to "live into" the wisdom emerging as the congregation turns toward wholeness.

Pastors, staff, and leadership should all be attending to their own self-care, and opportunities for respite need to be provided for any staff member who expresses a need for reflection and time away. For the whole church, congregational retreats, fellowship meals, and fun social events provide a place where pondering and play can intermingle during this last turn upward on the disaster trajectory, the turn toward wisdom. Memorial events can be staged at appropriate times: at the calendar marker, and additionally, at times more intuitively appropriate to the mood and movement of the congregation.

A return to congregational vitality may not be a linear or steady process; progress through reformation may be uneven, and this unevenness should not be resisted, nor should temporary "relapses" into disillusion or apathy be greeted with dismay or despair. They are a natural part of the phase of reforming, and their occurrence is to be treated matter-of-factly. As in the healing of the body after injury, tenderness remains, the well from which one draws strength and vitality takes time to refill, and the effects of trauma dwell in places least expected. Working through all of that in a holistic way takes time.

Among the leaders of one congregation that suffered a public violence event that took three lives, this season appeared in ways that were sometimes subtle, and other times abrupt and obvious.

Two months before the first anniversary, one of the associate pastors phoned his spiritual director. He told her he was feeling the need for a season of respite and didn't know what to do. He and another colleague had tended the congregation during the senior pastor's maternity leave, walking alongside the congregation through the early, difficult months of disillusionment. Now, though many in the congregation seemed to be advocating for a return to "normal," he and the other associate were feeling exhausted, drained, and adrift. The congregation had undertaken a complete renovation of the sanctuary where the murders had taken place. The pastor and faith community seemed restored to a sense of strength and were eagerly anticipating a planned rededication. But for these two, a restored sense of well-being seemed impossible to attain. Before reaching the Sunday that marked a year since the tragedy, one of the associate pastors resigned, and a month after the rededication service, the other associate left the church to enter a graduate program. It wasn't until nearly a year later that the pastor, too, began to express a sense of disconnection from the more restored sensibility of the congregation. During that long uneven season of reforming and change, a planned memorial sculpture remained unfinished in a sort of unplanned symbolic expression of the complexity of congregational recovery and reformation.

The second part of the Reformers' historic affirmation, *et semper reformanda,* "always reforming," is the place attained when the work of devastation, disillusionment, and reforming is integrated into understanding and practice. No longer do those who have been reformed by trauma maintain that faith is inviolable, or the world secure. Good people can become undone, evil exists and can strike the most vulnerable when least expected. And yet . . .

And yet, goodness and mercy can *still* follow us all the days of our life. Hope can be born out of chaos. The church that walks through the valley of the shadow together can become a potent witness to the power of the Light that shines in darkness, which the darkness cannot overcome. The congregation that learns this becomes a deeper, more real place for people to come who desperately need a true and honest faith, capable of sustaining in the dark valley.

This is not only a possibility for us but also the witness of our Scriptures. Using the Psalms, Walter Brueggemann describes the climb toward Wisdom as a "decisive move of faith . . . *from a context of disorientation* [Disillusionment] *to a new orientation* [Reforming], surprised by a new gift from God, a new coherence made present to us just when we thought all was lost [Wisdom]."[4]

This last move, "a departure from the 'pit' of chaos just when we had suspected we would never escape . . . is to be credited only to the intervention of God."[5] For those who survive the aftermath of violence and trauma, it is fundamentally Holy Mystery: a gift of goodness worked toward, but not achieved; watched for, but hidden in shadows, until its unexpected arrival surprises us with joy.

COMMUNITY-WIDE CARE

Restoration for a community affected by human-caused violence often begins with an intentional reclaiming of mission or purpose. The walk through the valley of the shadow finally comes to an end, and a new season in the life of the community emerges. After the heartache and struggle, the confusion and weariness, the disbelief and all the questions, a new or renewed sense of purpose and direction begins to take shape and direct the activities of the community. This (re)new(ed) sense of mission or purpose will look very different for each community.

For congregations, this process can be intentional and formalized, much like the process some congregations go through as they transition from one pastor to another. In some denominations, when a pastor leaves, an interim minister comes into a congregation to help them understand who they are, integrate the achievements of the past and make peace with perceived failures, discover their strengths and weaknesses, and discern God's invitation for the church's next season of life together. This interim process is intentional, specific, and geared toward moving the mission of the congregation forward into the future. Congregations affected by human-caused disasters and their pastoral leadership can also intentionally enter into a season of discernment. Following the steps of an interim process, they too can work toward renewing a sense of purpose and direction as a congregation that has survived a violent event. A renewed sense of identity and purpose begins to inform all that the congregation is and does.

It took us four years to get the energy back to where it was before the shooting. We had not planned on it taking that long—four years! When we sat with a consultant who walked us through an exercise where we built a timeline of activities and transitions, we were surprised at all the loss and grief we had experienced together. Some of it we acknowledged; much of it we just survived. It was hard work just to do our jobs and make it through one more week. We trudged on, doing our best. But then, in the fall of the fourth year after the incident, at the staff meeting following our Rally Day kick-off of the new church year, one of the staff members said, "We're finally back." We talked about "being back" and how hard the previous years had been. We talked about the hurts we endured and how we were different: as people, as a church, and as a staff working. And we talked about reclaiming our joy, or being reclaimed by joy. It had been a long time, a long walk through the valley of the shadow of death, but we realized at that staff meeting that we had made it through the valley—that particular valley—and we were now out of the shadows and in the sun. For the first time in years there was a group awareness of God's grace and goodness and light in ways that filled us with appreciation and joy.

WORSHIP

O LORD, my heart is not lifted up,
    my eyes are not raised too high;
I do not occupy myself with things
    too great and too marvelous for me.
But I have calmed and quieted my soul,
    like a weaned child with its mother;
    my soul is like the weaned child that is with me.

O Israel, hope in the LORD
    from this time on and forevermore.
                                        (Ps. 131:1–3)

Letting Begin, Letting Be, Letting Go

Even though it has been more than twenty years since the disaster that shattered the community where I served as pastor, I still remember the long months of sadness, depression, and listlessness in our church that seemed, at the time, unending. When the first anniversary of the event came around (though now we try to call them marker events rather than anniversaries) it was with great ambivalence that I began to plan the Sunday service. Though the national media seemed ready to proclaim victory and move on to the next tragedy, progress toward wholeness in our community was slow and unreliable. Some people in the church were evidencing classic signs of post-traumatic stress; in fact, even people who initially seemed less affected were suffering spiritual fallout as the months wore on. Parts of the community still felt depressed, anxious, weary, and sad. And yet, there was a continuing, though at times strained, affirmation of the reliable presence of God who, even in the valley of the shadow, was with us. By the end of the first year, we might have said we feared no evil, but there was such a long way yet to go. This much we were able to sing as we turned the corner from disillusion toward reforming: "grace hath brought us safe thus far, and grace will lead us home."

Letting Begin

In considering worship during this season of reforming, notice that the order of the rubrics, introduced in the guidance for worship in the aftermath of public violence, have been reversed. For the first Sundays after the impact of a human-caused disaster, the service was opened by *letting go*, a movement of relinquishment and lament. But in the two final phases of Reforming and Wisdom, the approach to worship is just the opposite. As lament completes its transformative work and begins to yield to wisdom, the people of God, while not exactly as they were before the event, *feel* more so. Before the disaster, they could enter a theater without dreading someone would begin shooting or sit down in worship without seeing blood in the chancel. During the work of disillusionment, there is an effortful, intentional choice made to embrace in worship the tension of lament and bring what has happened into sacred space. But in the phases of Reforming and Wisdom, there is a glimpse, at first far off, and then more nearly, of an *after*: a spiritual landscape ripening with the promise of goodness and mercy. The spiritual work of lament is nearing completion, and the turn toward wisdom has begun. So, instead of beginning by ending, reforming worship begins by beginning. The liturgy signals entrance into a place where still waters and green pastures beckon.

In the Jewish tradition, the end of the formal season of mourning after the death of a loved one is called a *Yahrzeit*. The liturgical tradition respects the power of loss, and makes generous space for mourning in the lives of survivors. During the first week following a death, the family stays at home, withdrawn from public life, tending to their loss, respecting its power, while friends and neighbors support them through gifts of presence, prayer, and food. As each month passes, in Sabbath worship, the names of the dead are spoken, and they and their families are lifted up in a prayer known as *kaddish*. The community does not place a memorial stone on the grave until a full year has passed. At the *Yahrzeit* service, prayers are offered to lift to God the mourners' remembrance, gratitude, and hope for the future. It is a liturgical marker event to conclude the formal first year of grieving and support the integration of loss; a ritual way of turning again toward wholeness, and the beginning of what we call the work of Reforming.

Letting Be

In the phase of Reforming, the importance of *letting be* in worship cannot be overstated. From the perspective of preaching, the more directive approach of the phase of Disillusionment, which addressed the explosion of old ways of understanding and explored the power of lament, can now begin to open up into a less structured kind of appreciative wondering.

This tentative, yet hopeful space can be framed spiritually through the liturgical observance of marker services or anniversaries in congregations that continue working their way through the impact of an act of public violence. A pastor of a church that lost its sexton and a church member when an armed intruder broke into the sanctuary recalled how his congregation addressed the one-year mark:

> *At the church, we chose to observe the anniversary of the event with a fellowship dinner and a special worship service. We decided to hold this service on the actual year marker of the event, rather than on the Sunday following. We met where we had met for worship a year ago, in the fellowship hall, since the sanctuary had been taped off by police and was unusable. The invitation to the congregation was given in this way: "It is . . . the sense of our staff and session that the church family needs such an opportunity (a* Yahrzeit*) to remember, to give thanks to God, to let go, and to go on with our common life, freed of the burden, if not wholly of the detritus, of the tragedy. Those of you who were with us for worship in the fellowship hall one year ago may remember that we said, 'What has happened to us, and what we tell of it, and make of it, will be our story, and the gift we offer to God. What is important to us remains, despite our losses. We will remember God's saving grace, always. . . .' We hope everyone who is part of the church community will remember, and join with us as we continue to bear witness to our story and God's presence."*

Symbolic action was, and continued to be, a very important way for that congregation to make meaning out of its loss and work of recovery. Because so many people were in different places—spiritually, emotionally, and physically—as the year marker date approached, they decided to celebrate Communion, and also to use a symbolic action that could be tailored to the individual needs of each participant. Though the anniversary of the tragedy had brought the entire community to a cross-place, the path each one would take out of that intersection was individual as well as communal.

During the prayers of confession, worshipers were given a piece of paper and invited to be in silence for a time, contemplating where they understood themselves to be along the journey toward healing and wholeness. Where were they still tender? What were their hopes? Using again the image of Lazarus as he stumbled from the tomb, the pastor asked what was still binding them, restraining them from new life? A quiet stillness settled on the congregation as they pondered, prayed, and wrote. After an extended period of silence, a deep metal bowl was brought into the chancel area, along with lighted candles and some incense. The pastor described how the honest prayers of any people are like incense, an offering that ascends to God. As the choir sang an anthem, the people were invited forward for a burning ceremony, to offer their fears, hopes, and prayers into God's keeping. Additionally, releasing the written prayers for burning served as an intentional choice for some in the congregation to begin their own turn toward reformation and wisdom.

The worship-work of reforming is, like the work of lament, an uneven and dynamic process. Sometimes the growth into healing and renewal will feel stable and linear—a steady ascent out of the deep and back up toward light and fresh air. But other times, the body can't move so quickly; or there has to be a pause, a waiting while breathing bodies catch up with intentions and hopes. In diving, too rapid of an ascent will cause the diver to experience the cramping, false euphoria and possible danger of the bends. The experienced diver knows that, no matter how ready she feels to be back up in the light, she must pause at various levels to adjust, so that the complete ascent can be accomplished safely. Worship and congregational life in the phases of Reforming and Wisdom are like that as well. It takes time to integrate the meaning of lament into personal awareness and communal understanding. It requires attentiveness as well as time to re-tie the strands of meaning, relationship, and understanding that were severed by the event. The pastor and congregation reforming toward wisdom should remain theologically and liturgically relaxed about the unevenness of the process. This is part of the unfinished story line of reforming, and the sense that things are "to be continued" is the beginning of wisdom. They must continue to follow the hose back up, and trust their progress, even when they find themselves needing to pause for a season, or even to back up a little. *Let be.* A healthy, whole body is what needs to be brought, by and by, into all that fresh air and light.

Letting Go

The second year after the trauma, when the anniversary Sunday approached, several members of the congregation's board asked, "Are we going to do that burning thing again this year?" They remembered how powerful it had been, on the anniversary of the event, to spend time in quiet contemplation, writing down those things by which they were still bound and burdened, and making of them a "burnt offering." They thought that doing it again would be good, since some people still remained affected by the violence. So, the second year, we did the burning thing again, and it felt fine . . . but I wondered—how long should this ritual continue? How will we know when it has served its purpose?

The third year came, and the worship committee asked, "Are we going to do the burning thing again?" To me, the ritual was starting to feel stale, but I wanted to respect the desires of the leadership. So I suggested that we might do the ritual this one more year, but shift its emphasis away from the event, and into a more general offering up of the sorts of ordinary things that bind us in our everyday lives. Perhaps one or two families in the congregation were still engaged in trauma recovery, but for the rest, the shift in content would signal our emergence into a place of restoration and wholeness.

When the Sunday came, I introduced the ritual in that way, moving it from the Confession to the Prayers of the People section of the worship order. Once again, people participated in the ritual, but this year, it felt, if not exactly flat, a little repetitive and predictable. I decided privately that I would resist doing it again, should they ask the following year; but they didn't. The reforming ritual had served its purpose, and in wisdom, we quietly and without fanfare let it go.

The process of reforming invites us to utilize such transitional rituals, but to take them lightly, recognizing that they are liminal expressions of a dynamic season in the church's life. Be willing to devise and use them, along with other specialized rituals of lament and healing; but be attentive to the energy the congregation invests in them. When that energy begins to shift or wane, take some time to consider where the congregation and its leaders are, and what expressions of ritual and liturgy can best serve on the way toward wisdom.

In some faith communities, there has been a resurgence of interest in the traditional spiritual disciplines. One practice many have come to find deeply meaningful is central to a spiritual tradition based on the teaching of Ignatius of Loyola. The practice, known as the Daily Examen, involves a daily commitment to an evening time of contemplation that explores, or examines, the events and feelings of the day just completed. One variation of the practice looks like this:

Stillness: Spend quiet moments relaxing into the presence of God.
Gratitude: Let yourself become thankful for the day just past, not seeking specific items to be grateful for, but seeing what rises in you as you reflect.
Reflection: Be present to the fullness of the day's experiences, paying attention to your emotions. Where did you sense the presence of God or experience consolation? Where did you notice the absence of God, or experience desolation?
Intention: Choose one feature of the day and pray from it.
Appreciation: Look toward tomorrow.

As a pastor and preacher moves through the season of Reforming with a worshiping congregation, using the Daily Examen for worship preparation week by week can be a rich way to engage a process of awareness (stillness and gratitude), assessment (reflection), advocacy (intention), and assurance (appreciation) as sermons and worship are crafted to guide the people's journey out of the valley of the shadow. Finally, we turn our attention to that place of green pastures and still waters that marks the way of wisdom.

7

Phase Four: Wisdom

About ten years ago, a congregation discovered that their youth direc-
tor had been abusing young women for several months. After one had
the courage to speak out and allegations were investigated, the direc-
tor was arrested. At first, the church leadership response appeared to
be swift, mostly behind the scenes. Whispers and rumors permeated the
community and some felt that things proceeded as if nothing had hap-
pened. In the months that followed, as the youth director was convicted,
imprisoned, and designated a sexual offender, the church called new
staff members and painfully began learning how to face, integrate, and
communicate their story.

By the end of the first year, unrest throughout the congregation
indicated a residue of trauma remaining from the lack of communally
addressed lament and healing. With the congregation, staff dedicated
itself to creating a more honest way forward. This response included
opportunities for the young women and their families to share their sto-
ries in safe ways, for the congregation to begin to articulate its own story
in ways that acknowledged senses of shame and sorrow for not having
been a safe place for the young women in the first place.

As the congregation moved through this work, their mission and
vision took renewed shape as well. In an effort to move beyond them-
selves, they created a center for abused youth. At first, this center and
their story took up significant portions of church-wide communication.
Gradually, it became just one significant part among many ministries of
the church. Today, this congregation enjoys increased membership with
a wide array of missions and outreach, as well as strong member care
and faith practices.

Finally, there is an "after" that marks emergence from the valley of
the shadow of death. Hope is renewed. A sense of energy and purpose
returns, turning the congregation and its members away from the internal work of trauma recovery and toward life beyond the boundaries of
grief. Green pastures unfold, and still waters refresh the spirit of those
who had been wounded and wandering.

There is mystery in the unfolding of this process. How congregations move through the four phases of human-caused disaster varies, depending on the characteristics and experiences of the congregation. After Devastation and Heroism, the slope of Disillusionment may vary greatly. Some move more quickly through this phase, while others, like the East Coast congregation mentioned above, take more time. Eventually, having moved through Disillusionment and after some months of being in the Reforming and recovery phase, the work of re-visioning and rebuilding continue and a sense of resolution emerges. In this time, congregational life feels steady and more reliably consistent. Many congregations experience an increasing sense of liveliness and joy. What some have called a "new normal" is not necessarily better than before—for assuredly, things are not how they used to be. So much is different, and the cost of trauma is real. Out of respect for that cost, this new normal can be alternatively described as a place of Wisdom. Like the other phases, Wisdom has both negative and positive connotations. Emerging into wisdom, a congregation and its leaders are no longer naive—if they ever were. They are fully aware of the impact and gravitas of life lost through violence. They know firsthand the far-reaching ripple effects of trauma, and how the impact of violence changes everything. Yet there is also a richness and sense of holy ground that comes from traversing the valley of the shadow of death together, and many have borne witness to a surprising joy that finds them along the way.

WISDOM MARKERS

It is impossible to describe with perfect detail precisely what "wisdom" looks like, on the far side of the valley of the shadow. The work of wisdom is incarnational: the Spirit molds pain and human resilience in unique and distinctive ways as congregations and their members move through their dark path, seeking the green pastures and quiet waters where God again is recognized as loving shepherd. Still, there are markers along the way, commonly experienced among those who have become members of this post-traumatic community of wisdom. They include:

Deeper Acceptance of Our Gifts and Limitations

For many, especially those whose work is that of caring for souls, "hitting bottom" when disillusionment and grief overwhelm all the work of heroic caring is a shattering experience. For many, the caring capabilities of professionals and the power of community have never been tried so sorely. To recognize that these gifts of love and caring are neither common nor inexhaustible, and therefore to recognize their preciousness and fragility, is a gift wisdom invites the healing survivor to embrace.

Gracious Acceptance of One's Failures and the Failures of Others

As individuals and systems come to embrace their own limitations following trauma with compassion, there is often a yielding up of shame and shaming—so often present in people of faith and their communities—into a more generous and gentle life together. People fail. Churches and their leaders fail. God's mercies are new every morning. God's faithfulness is great enough to reinvigorate a community with mercy and its people with tolerance and grace.

Living Out a New, Trauma-Informed Mission

After trauma, many congregations, like the one in the story that opened this chapter, find that their own experience of trauma and its aftermath have awakened in them a new sense of calling. Congregations may commit to active community leadership and advocacy against gun violence, or sexual abuse or trafficking. Members and leaders offer themselves as companions to others who fall victim to violence, or open their sanctuary's doors to shelter groups and individuals who work in trauma recovery. Sometimes, the new sense of mission may not relate directly to the experience of trauma and recovery, but be a new direction emerging with boldness out of a congregation that previously was cautious, but now, in the wake of trauma, sees itself as able to try new ideas and to embrace the unknown, together with its risks and rewards.

Embracing a Willingness to Serve Others

Many congregations previously preoccupied with self-care and survival experience the generosity and kindness of those who supported them in their crisis as an invitation to go and do likewise. The sense of self-containment and privacy that is peeled back by trauma and violence exposes both the vulnerability and the goodness of a community of faith to its neighbors; gratitude motivates a deep desire to give back.

More Sustainable Balance between Work and Self-Care

Trauma teaches moderation. Healing congregations learn the importance of pacing themselves, as healing is a marathon, not a sprint through the dark valley. They learn, by trial and error, how to balance the work of engaging recovery, in all its spiritual and emotional labor, with rest and space for integration, where the Spirit of God does the deep, invisible work, groaning alongside the suffering creation.

Freedom from Anxiety and a Playfulness and Lightness of Spirit

Faith work is serious and important, no more so than when matters of life and death are at stake. Those who survive trauma and find their way into wisdom often find, paradoxically, that they take themselves both more and less seriously at the same time.

They develop a deeper appreciation for liminality—the fragility and preciousness of life, and along with it, embrace the freedom that comes with accepting the limitations of human striving. Dame Julian of Norwich said, "All shall be well, and all shall be well, and all manner of thing shall be well."[1]

PASTORAL LEADERSHIP

For a pastor, wisdom lies in the willingness to integrate the process of moving from traumatic event to restoration into one's life and ministry, and into the life and ministry of the congregation. In the years of ministry that unfold long after trauma, it is not always clear that goodness and mercy have been present. Occasionally, though, awareness rises and there are glimpses of wisdom's grace:

> It was a simple and yet profound sentence. Years had passed since the violence occurred in the small church she served, and in the newsletter she wrote, "What brought us here, to this place, was the trauma." She was writing about the opening of a new congregational program for mentoring at-risk youth, a program for which that small congregation had raised significant funds. Long after the tragedy, they discovered that out of the "valley of the shadow of death" there is love to be shared and something amazing within reach; a way to be with others who, like them, had been hurting and were seeking to be healed.

Wisdom varies, and each pastor receives it in ways unique to her or him. For one it may be a fuller sense of possibility for the congregation. For another, it may be greater attunement to the more personal tragedies among members and families of the congregation. For another, it may be an expanded sense of vision and mission.

The experience of violence changes pastors. It changes the filters and lenses through which they view their lives, their congregations, and the world around them. A pastor's sense of call often alters in the aftermath of violence. This is natural. Pastors should embrace the potential of change and growth, and not be afraid to share their wisdom and experience, or explore new avenues of engagement in ministry. It is helpful when such leaders share their process of growth with staff and lay members. Trust that growth and healing that has unfolded will prove effective in ways never before imagined.

STAFF AND LAY EXPERIENCES

In the two years after a mass shooting, the intern at the time of the incident was ordained and became the youth pastor of the local congregation where she had served her internship. Though the aftermath had been intense and relentless with the pressure of grief and overwhelming need, the pastor, staff, and lay leaders had become a strong team, encouraging one another in their self-care and supporting how each of them led their respective ministry areas. The youth pastor consistently demonstrated her strengths in facilitating gatherings that were emotionally safe opportunities for youth and parents to express their grief, wrestle with their sense of God's presence, and seek hope together amid their heartache. Her leadership and shepherding were experienced as a strong anchor for those families. In this church, interns tended to come and go—not become one of the new pastors. As the youth pastor continued to expand her capabilities, she was noticed by church governing leaders, and soon called to become the lead pastor of another church. Her present church celebrated with her, confirming the sense of calling that she felt and practiced, and they had experienced.

In the aftermath of violence, the wisdom expressed by staff and members of the congregation gives shape to a deepening sense of vocational mission and ministry. They are ready to participate in the new life of the church community in ways that speak to the full scope of life with which they are now familiar. Looking back at where they have come from, and having faced their corporate sorrow, they have a greater communal sense of how the mourner's path is an asset along life's journey. For some this is a new realization, for others, a reminder of what they have already known.

For some, the skills gained in learning to grieve and heal from a more recent violent event can open the possibility to revisit violence in the past that may not have received sufficient care and attention. It can be a time of healing long-standing wounds in the collective story of the congregation. When the process from impact through reforming is one of honesty and communal movement toward health, members discover their congregation to be truly a sanctuary and safe haven amid life's many other storms.

Visitors and members of congregations in the season of Wisdom find the church to be a place of learning and renewal; a place that does not shy away from harsher realities, but instead faces them with grace, gentleness, and perseverance. Staff members, who have not burned out or become entrenched in the exhaustion of compassion fatigue, find that their strengths and abilities fit the broad range of care and leadership that congregations require throughout their life trajectories. People often find that there are certain relationships that have stood the test of time and borne the weight and stresses inherent in the course of healing after violence. The bonds formed in these months and years can last a lifetime. Most of all, in the season of Wisdom, staff and members discover they have deep internal wells of strength and compassion to create and sustain ministries and programs that meet congregants in the heartache and joy of their lives. If they did not before, staff and members find they have the courage to participate in congregational practices that express their faithfulness as they yearn to share honest human experiences in genuine encounters with the divine presence.

CONGREGATIONAL CARE

As survivors of public violence emerge from the valley of the shadow that was encompassed by sorrow, anger, and loss, *how* congregations were supported throughout their descent into the season of lament and disillusionment matters. If informed by a conviction that God was with them as they went *below*, then it is likely that such support makes it possible to begin the hopeful ascent toward wisdom. There is transformation for those who would embrace the totality of life's experiences, a

gift of newness that remakes utterly the world that once was. This is not
a return to the original, perhaps naive perspective, for there can be no
going back to where we were *before*. Poet Mary Oliver observed, "Belief
isn't always easy / But this much I have learned— / if not enough
else— / to live with my eyes open."[2] Recovery establishes a place of
goodness that can tolerate disappointment or distress and find courage
to endure. This resolution is symbolized on the chart in the introduction by a differentiation of level between the pre-trauma reality and
recovery, the place we call Wisdom: not a lesser state, but rather, a place
closer to the earth, more human than before.

In Wisdom, God's gracious and transforming work is acknowledged
and celebrated. A new sense of belonging and possibility for the believer
is articulated. The safety now felt by those who sing a new song is not
rooted in a secure or predictable world, or in the solidity of doctrines,
but rather, in a serene confidence that, in whatever circumstances, life
belongs to God. The faith community is rooted in that identity, as one
of God's own. And so the psalmist sings, "You have turned my mourning into dancing; you have taken off my sackcloth and clothed me with
joy, so that my soul may praise you and not be silent" (Ps. 30:11–12).

COMMUNITY-WIDE CARE

In the fourth and final phase of a human-caused disaster response the
community appears to be back to normal—life continues to move forward. Still, the community never quite gets back to the way things
were before the traumatic event. Ordinary life reasserts its reassuring
rhythms, shaped by a deeper, more reflective and appreciative outlook
on life. The mayor of one community, devastated by the loss of several
firefighters in an arson fire, reported:

> *I never drive by the fire station without saying a prayer. When I see
> members of the fire department at the grocery store or at a youth soccer
> game there is now a hug when before it would have been a handshake.
> We don't talk about what happened very much, but we are aware of
> what happened, thankful to have lived through it, and learned that our
> lives can be taken from us at any moment. I think we have grown to
> appreciate the privilege of simply being in community together.*

The collective experiences of the community to rally together, to
grieve, to struggle to do the best they could, to recognize they have

survived, and to continue to do what needs to be done day in and day out are the strands from which wisdom is woven. Having survived a traumatic event and lived through the response, the community now has a deeper sense of the fragility of life, the impact of evil and loss, and the joyfulness of being alive together. A community matures in the ways it operates, the purpose toward which it strives, and the way its members interact with one another.

In the aftermath of an incident at the high school, the ministerial alliance in the community changed everything about its monthly meetings. Instead of being focused on supporting the community food drive or figuring out the schedule for the baccalaureate service, pastors now gather to support one another. They have become friends, colleagues in ministry, who meet to tend to the soul of the community by paying attention to one another's souls. They have learned that the most important thing they can offer the community is to be attentive to their own wellness first and then take care of business. And to be honest, a lot of the time, they never get to the business.

Surviving trauma offers an invitation to evaluate old ways of doing business: the way public meetings are conducted, the way people greet one another at the grocery store, the things to which precious time and attention are given. Some of the "old ways" no longer make sense in the aftermath of a traumatic event; new ways, wise ways, begin to emerge and guide the life of the community.

WORSHIP

Three years after the trauma, one of the final pieces of brokenness remaining from the event was about to unfold—divorce. The cost of the violence and its aftermath on the pastoral family, and the resultant compassion fatigue, had strained relationships to the breaking point, and the copastor couple was about to announce they had, through counseling and prayer, reached a decision to end their marriage. The week before the announcement, a guest preacher arrived in town and was picked up at the airport. After hugging the younger woman, the visiting preacher exclaimed, "You look awful! What's wrong?" The copastor replied, "It's just that we are about to announce that we are getting a divorce . . . and the congregation already went through so much with the shooting . . . and I have no idea what they are going to do when we tell them. . . . I'm so afraid, and I just wish it would go away."

The older woman put her arms around her now weeping friend.
"Look at me," she said. "When you tell the truth about yourself in church,
other people learn they can tell the truth, too, and church becomes an
entirely different place. Tell the truth, and your people will love you for
it, and church will become a place where truth and love abide."

Though this may seem a strange place to begin a section on how wisdom is expressed in the worship life of a congregation that has finally reached the green pastures of wholeness after trauma, it is the purest distillation of all the wisdom gained from walking alongside traumatized congregations and their pastors after the violence of human-caused disaster: tell the truth about yourself, and other people will learn they can tell the truth, too. Tell the truth in church, and church becomes a safe place, a place alive with love and wisdom. In ministry, learning to tell the truth in church transforms persons as pastors and as human beings. It brings a new vitality into the worship life of a congregation, opening up sacred space so that others, members and friends, can begin to explore their whole spiritual selves in church as well. As pastoral leaders learn to embrace this wisdom, they may find themselves surprisingly willing and able to ask many other questions in church too, questions many may feel are somehow off limits to traditional mainline congregations. For example,

— Why do we pray a prayer of confession? I don't feel so much lost in sin as I feel confused by all the wrongness in the world.
— Why can't you preach a sermon on why the Bible doesn't have to be literally true?
— Why do we say, "Lord, you hear our prayers" in the Prayers of the People when some of us find it hard to believe that God intervenes in a personal way in our circumstances?
— Why do we thank God when we are spared from the effects of a hurricane, when someone else's community just got hit? Do we think God is blessing us and cursing them? Why don't we blame God when something horrific happens?

As the congregation begins to realize they have developed the resilience and strength to ask and explore anything together, pastors and other leaders discover they have lost that haunting fear of failure, the desperate need for the approval of others, the insistence that everything stay just as it has always been. When people learn to tell the truth in church, many who have quietly kept their questions and their passions to themselves will begin stepping up and speaking up, finding their voices and strengthening the life of the congregation.

Communities of faith and their leaders can learn through trauma that truth-telling in worship is an art that is possible, necessary, and a potent force in the healing process. Congregations that painfully reform their common life and liturgy through practicing the work of lament arrive at a place where worship feels like wisdom's house, like home. Without the gift of wisdom brought forth by devastation, disillusionment, and reforming, many congregations would never have found the courage to become the congregations they and their pastors once dreamed of being. And that is both a blessing and a challenge.

Why do we wait for the worst to happen before we stop taking worship—and its amazing capacity to touch and transform our lives through symbol, song, word, and ritual—for granted? Why would we need a traumatic shattering of our faith-world in order to examine carefully each element of worship, to see how they can vibrantly evoke and truthfully reflect the complex realities of our lives and our world?

Doing Worship from a Place of Wisdom

What is suggested as best practice for congregational worship in the new normal of Wisdom is to deepen and treat as normative the processes that have been offered in the foregoing chapters. Never take the order of service for granted again! Don't just plug in prayers from some book of liturgy, or pull illustrations off the Internet, or go through the motions by rote. Now that preacher and congregation have tasted the astonishing healing and reforming power of truth in church, never be satisfied to go back to what was before. Artful worship, thoughtful, connected worship, is a gift to pastor and congregation alike. Familiar, ancient words and rituals can be infused with deeper meaning. Taking the time for planning worship *every* week with openness, curiosity, and intentionality is a spiritual discipline, a practice that will be spiritually enriching as well as keep the worship experience vital for the congregation. If engaging these practices during the stressful and chaotic season following disaster is both possible and desirable, how much more so will it be during ordinary days and seasons?

Returning to the treatment of "Worship Reimagined" in chapter 2, consider once again the questions of each movement in worship—this time, from the place of wisdom and within the blessing of still waters and green pastures. Take time weekly to practice a kind of "daily exa-men" for congregational worship, with movements of stillness, grati-tude, reflection, intention, and appreciation.

Stillness: Spend quiet moments relaxing into the presence of God.

Gratitude: Let yourself become grateful for the life of the congregation, and the daily blessings and birthings of life within a congregational community.

Reflection: Be present to the fullness of life in faith, and the life of the wider community, paying attention to your emotions. Where did you sense the presence of God or experience consolation? Where did you notice the absence of God or experience desolation?

Intention: Let something that feels true, resonant, and meaning-full rise into your consciousness. Ponder and play with it. Will it preach? How can you invite the congregation's awareness and engagement by the way you craft worship?

Appreciation: Know that life is good. Appreciate the companionship you have had, from God and from others, in the valley of the shadow and at the Table where blessing overflows. Be grateful, whatever comes.

A WITNESS COMING TO WISDOM

It seems fitting that the last words be spoken by those who have walked through the fires of violence and trauma, and found their way to wisdom.

I continue to move toward greater peacefulness and joy in life and in ministry, what I now call "wisdom." The last several years have been hard, especially dealing with the personal trauma of the shooting inci-dent, the vocational trauma the event caused in my sense of purpose and the trajectory of my ministry, and the weariness I continue to feel at issues that now seem ridiculously unimportant. I continue to work with a counselor, a spiritual director, and others in an effort to discern what God is inviting me to be and do. I continue to refine a new sense of "nor-mal," one that appropriates the experiences of the past six years and looks to the future with hope. I've also come to see life as a "gift of the Spirit," the breath of life, and that our invitation is to live the gift, share the gift, and enjoy the gift. I have a much deeper appreciation for the limits of life and the awareness that it could all blow away way before I plan on it ending. There is something both terrifying and liberating about this.

Regula Vitae

I too will die,
so now is a time to live.
Now is a time to suffer
and love and serve and learn.
Now is a time to laugh
and cry and mourn and rejoice.
Now is a time to walk in the woods
and splash in a stream
and cook dinners with joy.
Now is a time to love well,
to pay attention,
to care for myself
and to offer thanks.
Now is a time to live
because I too will die.
I choose life!
I will
cherish quiet
cultivate love
pay attention
make fun
eat well
walk slowly
accept failings
say 'no'
live small
be closer to the ground
learn gently
offer thanks
recognize distractions
serve others
trust grace
be-loved and
be as well as I can be!
                    —David Holyan

APPENDIXES
Worship Resources

Appendix 1
Prayers in the Midst of Trauma

A Prayer for Those Present after a Traumatic Event

God of our life, whose presence sustains us in every circumstance, in the aftermath of terror and loss, we seek the grounding power of your love and compassion. We open our hearts in anger, sorrow, and hope; that those who have been spared as well as those whose lives are changed forever may find solace, sustenance, and strength in the days of recovery and reflection that come.

We pray in grief, remembering the lives that have been lost and maimed, in body or spirit.

We ask for sustaining courage for those who are suffering; strength and skill for those who are working to save and heal, in body and spirit. In these moments of shock and sorrow, open our eyes, our hearts, and our hands to the movements of your Spirit, who flows in us like the river whose streams make glad the city of God and the hearts of all who dwell in it and in you.

In the name of Christ, our healer and our light, we pray. Amen.

A Prayer after an Event of Public Violence, for Pastors and Staff Supporting Others

God our shelter,
> hold us under the shadow of your wings as we bow before you in grief and pain.

We pray for each family who has lost a beloved child, a mother, a friend;
we pray for those who have witnessed horror, and are wounded in body or spirit,
for each of them is a child made in your image.

We pray for ourselves, that we will find strength to support the brokenhearted,
grace to find our way in the darkness of grief, anger, and loss;
light to sense your presence, even in the valley of the shadow of death.
Restore our hopes, our hearts,
even as we weep with grief and tremble with anger.

Fill us, your wounded, willing people, with a peace that passes
   understanding,
the courage to nurture healing and hope,
and the willingness to bear the Christ-light, even in these days of
   shadow.
In the name of Jesus, we pray. Amen.

A Prayer in the Hospital

Merciful God—
   whose presence hovers over us and all our troubled world,
   whose Spirit intercedes for us with groanings too deep for human
      utterance—
help us now.
We are heartbroken, frightened, and angry.
We can scarcely believe how abruptly horror and violence have shattered
   our lives.
Be with us as we endure these anxious, endless moments of waiting . . .
   give us strength and courage to bear the unknown.
Let us know your sustaining grace, and feel the touch of your hand
   in the touch of neighbors and friends.
Hover over our loved ones with healing grace and peace.
Guide the hands and the hearts of medical professionals as they work to save.
May those who have been injured
   know that you are near, have respite from pain and horror,
      and see your light, even in the midst of darkness.
May our prayers be acceptable to you,
   and our tears a beginning of a balm to suffering souls.
In the name of the Christ we pray. Amen.

A Prayer after Mass Terror

God of mercy, whose presence sustains us in every circumstance, in the
midst of unfolding violence and the aftermath of terror and loss, we seek
the grounding power of your love and compassion.

   In these days of fearful danger and division, we need to believe somehow that your kindom of peace—in which all nations and tribes and lan-
guages dwell together in peace—is still a possibility. Give us hope and
courage, so that we might not yield our humanity to fear, even in these
endless days of dwelling in the valley of the shadow of death.

   We pray for neighbors in (*location of terror attack*) who, in the midst of
the grace of ordinary life—while at work, or at play—have been violently

assaulted, their lives cut off without mercy. We are hostages of fear, caught in an escalating cycle of violence whose end cannot be seen. Free us from fear, that we may be instruments of your peace

We open our hearts in anger, sorrow, and hope. May those who have been spared as well as those whose lives are changed forever find solace, sustenance, and strength in the days of recovery and reflection that come. We give thanks for strangers who comfort the wounded and who welcome stranded strangers, for first responders who run toward the sound of gunfire and into the smoke and fire of bombing sites.

We ask for sustaining courage for those who are suffering; for wisdom and diligence among global and national agencies and individuals assessing threat and directing relief efforts; and for our anger and sorrow to unite in service to the establishment of a reign of peace, where the lion and the lamb may dwell together, and terror will not hold sway over our common life. In these days of shock and sorrow, open our eyes, our hearts, and our hands to the movements of your Spirit, who flows in us like the river whose streams make glad the city of God and the hearts of all who dwell in it and in you.

In the name of Christ, our healer and our light, we pray. Amen.

Appendix 2
Hymns

GOD, WE'VE KNOWN SUCH GRIEF AND ANGER
Carolyn Winfrey Gillette   IN BABILONE

God, we've known such grief and anger
As we've heard your people cry
We have asked you, "How much longer?"
We have sadly wondered why.
In this world of so much suffering
May we hear your word anew:
I will never leave you orphaned,
I will not abandon you.

By your grace comes resurrection
By your love you cast out fear.
You give strength and sure direction
As we seek to serve you here.
You give comfort to the grieving,
and you bless the ones who mourn.
May we trust in you, believing,
out of chaos, hope is born.

Hope is ours for, God, you love us,
You have claimed us by your grace.
And through steadfast love you call us
To bring hope to every place.
In each rescue worker's caring,
In each faithful volunteer,
In each person's love and sharing,
God, we glimpse your kingdom here.

THROUGH CLOUD AND OUT OF CHAOS: A HYMN FOR A HARD SEASON

Laurie Ann Kraus   ES IST EIN ROS 7.6.7.6.6.7.6*

O, God of Hosts, restore us.
Turn toward us in your grace.
Stir up your might and save us,
Teach us to seek your face.
> Your people cry in pain.
> Bereft, adrift, and longing:
> God, make us whole again.

Come, God of present danger,
Return, and guide us home.
Speak to us, Friend and Stranger:
We trust in you alone.
> We watch and work and pray,
> The Spirit's life revealing
> To wait the coming day.

Through cloud and out of chaos
Your people speak your Name.
In darkness, God will stay us,
A path toward light to frame.
> Toward hope our hearts are drawn
> Your healing life abounding,
> Your love, our steadfast song.

*Sung to the tune of "Lo, How a Rose E'er Blooming."

Appendix 3
Vesper and Community Vigil Services

In the wake of a community tragedy, people want to be together to pray and to grieve. If possible, a service the evening of the tragedy or the day after is very helpful. Many also want to gather more frequently in the first days after a traumatic event. Services are often held in the church, community center, or the site of the event. Following are two services that can be used for these purposes, one more structured, the other more informal.

A VESPER SERVICE FOR HEALING AND WHOLENESS

Gathering Words

(As these words are read, light candles throughout the sanctuary, especially on the Table.)

Sometimes we experience such darkness that we lose all our energy. But our intent in life is to continue to live in God and faithfully trust that we will be shown compassion and grace. This is God's own working in us. Out of the goodness of God the eye of our understanding is opened by which we see, sometimes more and sometimes less, according to the ability we are given to receive. As Jesus revealed to Dame Julian of Norwich, "It was necessary that there should be sin; but all shall be well, and all shall be well, and all manner of thing shall be well."[1]

Call to Prayer

Cantor: My shepherd, you supply my need, Beloved is your name.
  In pastures fresh you make me feed, beside the living stream.
  You bring my wand'ring spirit back, when I forsake your ways . . .
  You lead me, for your mercy's sake, in paths of truth and grace.
One: O Lord, open my lips—
All: **And my mouth shall proclaim your praise.**

Song "Precious Lord, Take My Hand," Thomas A. Dorsey

Prayer of Confession (Augustine of Hippo)[2]

O Lord our God,
    let the shelter of your wings give us hope.
Protect us and uphold us.
You will be the Support that upholds
    from childhood till the hair on our heads is grey.
When you are our strength we are strong,
    but when our strength is our own we are weak.
In you our good abides forever,
    and when we turn away from it we turn to evil.
Let us come home at last to you, O Lord,
    for fear that we will be lost.
For in you our good abides and it has no blemish,
    since it is yourself.
Nor do we fear that there is no home to which we can return.
We fell from it;
    but our home is your eternity
    and it does not fall because we are away.

Assurance of Grace (based on Psalm 126)

When the Lord restores the exiles to Zion, it will seem like a dream. Then our mouths will fill with laughter, our tongues with joyful song. Then they will say among the nations, "The Lord has done great things for them." It is for us that the Lord is doing great things; we will rejoice. Lord, restore our fortunes, as streams revive the desert. Then those who sow in tears shall reap in joy. Those who go forth weeping, bearing sacks of seeds, shall come home with shouts of joy, bearing their sheaves.

Sharing the Peace of Christ

As Christ has welcomed us, so let us welcome one another.
Let us share God's peace with our neighbors.

Psalm 131

O LORD, my heart is not lifted up.
    my eyes are not raised too high;
I do not occupy myself with things
    too great and too marvelous for me.

But I have calmed and quieted my soul,
  like a weaned child with its mother;
  my soul is like the weaned child that is with me.

[So may my heart be.]
O Israel, hope in the LORD
  from this time on and forevermore.

Invitation to Stillness

Let us be still, held by the presence of God.
Let us wait with hope, to see what Holy Mystery unveils.

(Silence may be kept. If it is comfortable for the congregation, as much as several minutes of silence can be calming and healing.)

One: Christ, the light of the world, comes to dispel the darkness in our
  hearts.
**All: So like the first disciples, who cradled sorrow in the long dark
  before Easter day, we wait in faith and prayer: for ourselves, for
  those we love, and for those who have been lost.**

Song   "God of Compassion, in Mercy Befriend Us" (O QUANTA QUALIA)

  or

  "Amazing Grace/My Chains Are Gone," Chris Tomlin

Reading   Revelation 21:1–5a or Job 23:1–17

Meditation

(A brief meditation may be shared, based on the text from Revelation, focusing on the realities of grief and sorrow in our experience and our world, together with the hope that God, who knows our suffering, will one day dry our tears and end the sorrow of death. Another approach is to address directly the anger and sorrow and sense of God's absence that strike us after violence and loss. For this approach, use the text from Job.)

Silence

Song   "Jesus, Remember Me," Jacques Berthier (REMEMBER ME)

Intercessions

(The following prayer may be offered as a pastoral prayer, as free community prayers, or as bidding prayers; with the presider inviting the community to prayer for those killed or wounded, for their families and those who grieve, offering thanksgiving for first responders and medical personnel, praying for strength and wisdom for the congregation and the larger community, and for peace and healing.)

God of our life, whose presence sustains us in every circumstance, in the aftermath of terror and loss, we seek the grounding power of your love and compassion. We open our hearts in anger, sorrow, and hope: that those who have been spared as well as those whose lives are changed forever may find solace, sustenance, and strength in the days of recovery and reflection that come.

Once again, Holy One, we cry, "How long, O Lord?" We wonder when will it be enough? We grieve the continued erosion of the fabric of our common life, the reality of fear that warps the common good. We pray in grief, remembering the lives that have been lost and maimed, in body or spirit.

We ask for sustaining courage for those who are suffering; for wisdom and diligence among agencies and individuals assessing threat and directing relief efforts; and for our anger and sorrow to unite in service to the establishment of a reign of peace, where the lion and the lamb may dwell together, and terror will not hold sway over our common life.

In these days of shock and sorrow, open our eyes, our hearts, and our hands to the movements of your Spirit, who flows in us like the river whose streams make glad the city of God and the hearts of all who dwell in it and in you.

In the name of Christ, our healer and our light, we pray. Amen.

The Lord's Prayer

Anointing with Oil

(Invite those who wish to come forward to stations for anointing and prayer. A meditative piece, perhaps something from the Taizé or Iona community, might be used as background during the anointing.)

Song "You Shall Be Like a Garden," J. Philip Newell

Benediction

COMMUNITY VIGIL OUTLINE

This service outline can be used for both a community-based vigil or a gathering in the church for the community of faith.

Setting: dark, with unlit candles distributed to those gathered. Leaders process in silence or to music appropriate to both the situation and the community.

Welcome

(Offered by the person perceived to have the most authority)

Prayer of Invocation

(Have someone light a single, large candle as this prayer is offered.)

Gracious God, we gather here shocked and hurting.
> The news of this day has ripped our hearts and torn our souls.
> We find ourselves walking through the valley of the shadow of death.
> We have found ourselves walking in the darkness of disbelief and sorrow.
> We have found ourselves walking in the dark, unsure of your presence with us.
> We are here, before you, in the darkness of our pain, our hurt, our anger . . .
> We gather here, in the darkness of our loss of _____ (*name the loss or victims*).
> We gather here in support of _____ (*name surviving family members*).
> Lord God, be with us now in this darkness.
> Be with us now in this hurt and pain.
> Be with us now as we shed our tears and offer our prayers.

> Gracious and loving God, be with us now, in all we do.
> In Jesus' name we pray. Amen.

(A leader lights a candle from the one big candle and then lights the candles of a few people, who in turn share the light with others assembled. Let this take time, and don't rush to the next element in the service.)

Opening Reading   Psalm 130

Instrumental Music (optional)

Ritualized Prayer

(After the reading of Psalm 130, have two people offer prayers for the victims, survivors, families, congregation, and community.)

Speaker One: I wait for the Lord, my soul waits, and in God's word I hope.
Speaker Two: Lord, in our waiting, we pray for *(offers a petition)*.

Speaker One: *(Repeat the refrain when the petition is complete)* **I wait for the Lord, my soul waits, and in God's word I hope.**
Speaker Two: Lord, in our waiting, we pray for *(offers another petition)*.

(Continue in this way, leaving a good amount of time for quiet reflection at the end.)

Closing Reading   Psalm 130

(You may want to use a different reading here, but it is nice to have the same reading offered as a container for all the emotional and spiritual energy that is swirling through the community. You might begin the reading by saying: "Let us hear again the Word of the Lord.")

Benediction

We worship a God who offers steadfast love and redemption to all.
One who redeems us from all iniquity and pain;
One who comfort and consoles;
One who is our light, shining forth in the midst of the darkness.
May God's light shine, now, and in the days ahead. Amen.

Postlude (optional)

(Leaders recess out of the liturgical space.)

Appendix 4
Sunday Service after Violence

GATHERING

Prelude

Choral Introit   "By the Waters of Babylon"

Call to Worship   (inspired by Psalm 1)

> One: Happy are those who do not follow the advice of the wicked,
> or take the path that sinners tread, or sit in the seat of scoffers.
> **All: Lord, this day we have tasted the bitter fruit of wickedness.**

> One: Our delight is in the law of the Lord,
> and on God's law we meditate day and night.
> **All: Our hearts are broken, our minds filled with disbelief.
> Through our grief we ask, "Where were you?"**

> One: We are like trees planted by streams of water,
> which yield their fruit in season,
> our leaves do not wither.
> **All: Let our worship be for us streams of living water.
> Sustain the faithfulness of your community.
> In the face of all we have endured, let us not wither!**

> One: Let us prosper in our worship of the Lord!

Hymn   "We Come to You for Healing, Lord" (LAND OF REST)

Prayer of Confession

God of peace, we confess to you this day that we are hurting, angry, and confused. In our moment of need, did you leave us? How did you let this happen? Our hearts are broken with grief and loss. Unsure of where to turn for comfort and strength, we gather here . . . and wait. We wait for your goodness, your hope, and your peace to appear once again. Be with us in our waiting. Be with us as we hurt. Bear gently our anger. Walk with us through our confusion. Be our peace, this day and forevermore. Amen.

Silence for Personal Prayer

Invitation to Restoration "Don't Be Afraid" (IONA)

(This may be sung by one voice, then repeated by the entire congregation.)

Assurance of Pardon

The peace of our God surpasses understanding. The peace of our God clears away fear. The peace of our God renews our strength and guides our hearts as we seek to be faithful in all we do—even this, even now. Sisters and brothers, hear again the good news of Jesus Christ offered to you and to all people: "Peace I leave with you; my peace I give to you. I do not give to you as the world gives. Do not let your hearts be troubled, and do not let them be afraid" (John 14:27).

Sharing the Peace of God

(Please share the peace of Christ with your neighbors.)

PONDERING

Prayer of Illumination

Psalm of Restoration (based on Psalm 126)

When the Lord restores the exiles to Zion, it will seem like a dream. Then our mouths will fill with laughter, our tongues with joyful song. Then they will say among the nations, "The Lord has done great things for them." It is for us that the Lord is doing great things; we will rejoice. Lord, restore our fortunes, as streams revive the desert. Then those who sow in tears shall reap in joy. Those who go forth weeping, bearing sacks of seeds, shall come home with shouts of joy, bearing their sheaves.

Reading from the Hebrew Scriptures Isaiah 61:1–4

Reading from the New Testament Romans 8:18–27

Sermon

Response "I Will Come to You (You Are Mine)," David Haas

PRACTICING

Pastoral Prayer

The Lord's Prayer

The Offering

The Offertory

Doxology

SHARING IN THE TABLE OF GRACE

The Sacrament of Holy Communion

Communion Invitation

Lord, we come to this table, a community broken and shaken. We struggle to make sense out of the events of the last (*days/hours*). We struggle to recognize your presence. We struggle with the enormity of our hurt and pain. Lord, we are struggling! And in the midst of our struggle, in the midst of our hurt, in the midst of our pain, we come here, to this table, your supper. We come needing grace and mercy. We come needing love and care. We come needing comfort and strength. We come, this day, dear Lord, with a lot of needs on our hearts and in our souls.

Yet Lord, we come to this table, mindful also of the mysteries of your presence in the breaking of bread and the sharing of the cup—your body broken, your blood shed. We gather this day in the shadow of death, knowing only too well the sense of your absence in the midst of broken bodies and shed blood. We wonder: are you really here, now, with us? We gather, seeking the mystery of your transforming grace; your brokenness feeds us, your blood redeems us. May these simple elements, the bread we are about to break and the cup we are about to fill, be a blessing for us all. May we remember that in the breaking of the bread you welcome us into a life-giving fellowship with you and all the saints throughout time. And may we remember that in the sharing of the cup our sins are forgiven, and we are offered grace upon grace yet again. Be with us now, in this sacred meal, and remind us all of your goodness and grace.

Thanksgiving

The Lord be with you.
And also with you.
Lift up your hearts.
We lift them up to the Lord.
Let us give thanks to the Lord our God.
It is right to give our thanks and praise.
Even in the midst of tragedy, we praise you, God,
    for your Spirit brooded over chaos,
    separated light from darkness,
    and brought order and breathed life, calling it "very good."
Despite the brokenness and chaos that envelop us,
    we still believe your Spirit is at work,
        breathing peace,
        stilling the storm,
        bringing life out of death.
Send down your Holy Spirit upon us,
    and upon these, your gifts of bread and wine.
May what is common be holy,
    for the fellowship of this, your Table of grace.
May the bread that is broken mend our shattered souls.
May the cup of Christ's new covenant slake our thirst for mercy and peace.
May we, who join at this Table, be nourished and strengthened
        to be your healing presence in the world,
        and shine as light in the midst of darkness.
Therefore we gladly join our voices
    in the song of the saints and the church
    on earth and in heaven, saying:

Holy, holy, holy Lord,
God of power and might;
Heaven and earth are full of your glory.
Hosanna in the highest.
Blessed is the One who comes in the name of the Lord.
Hosanna in the highest.

Breaking the Bread and Pouring the Cup

Sharing the Meal

Singing as You Come to the Table   "Come to the Table of Grace,"
Barbara Hamm

or

"Taste and See," James E. Moore Jr.

Prayer of Thanksgiving

Holy God, we thank you for the simple comfort of a meal with friends.

We bless you for your presence in our midst; you, who walked a way of suffering among us, and who was resurrected by Love. We offer ourselves in the service of your mercy, your healing grace, and your peace. Give us strength, give us endurance, and feed us with your Spirit of hope even as we have been fed at your Table. In the name of the Christ we pray. Amen.

Hymn   "Through Cloud and Out of Chaos: A Hymn for a Hard Season," Laurie Ann Kraus

(See appendix 2, p. 119.)

Benediction

Appendix 5
First Year Marker Service (Anniversary)

REMEMBERING

Prelude

(Distribute pencils and slips of paper for the prayers to be written during the Silent Prayer.)

Welcoming the Light

(Light candles as this prayer is read.)

This is the time of ending,
   and the time of beginning again.
This is the time of being,
   and of being known by God.
This is the season for remembering,
   and for being remembered by God.
In our endings, our beginnings,
   In remembering, and being re-membered
      To one another and to God—
The Lord of hosts is with us, and the God of light is our refuge.

Call to Worship   (based on Psalm 126)

When the Lord restores the exiles to Zion, it will seem like a dream. Then our mouths will fill with laughter, our tongues with joyful song. Then they will say among the nations, "The Lord has done great things for them." It is for us that the Lord is doing great things; we will rejoice. Lord, restore our fortunes, as streams revive the desert. Then those who sow in tears shall reap in joy. Those who go forth weeping, bearing sacks of seeds, shall come home with shouts of joy, bearing their sheaves.

Hymn   "God, We've Known Such Grief and Anger," Carolyn
Winfrey Gillette

(See appendix 2, p. 118.)

Scripture Reading   Psalm 23

Prayer of Confession

God of grace and peace, God of beginnings and endings, look upon us,
and hear our prayer. In this season of remembering, we acknowledge to
you our brokenness, our anger, our emptiness. We do not want always to
look backward with regret, but we are uncertain how to move forward.
We want vengeance, we want relief. We want things to be the way they
were. We want to be sure you are on our side. We want to be more, to be
better than we are. Help us to let go of that which holds us back; help us
to remember for good, as you have remembered us. For we know, God
our life, that you have made all peoples by your love, and that you call
every creature by name. Help us to find ourselves and our place in your
purposes for creation. Teach us to find ways to live together in unity.
Fill us with courage, with hope, and with peace. Help us to begin again.
Amen.

Assurance of Pardon

Call to Remembrance

(Here, names of those who were lost may be read.)

Silent Prayer

*(During the silence, small votive candles might be lighted for each life lost or in
a symbolic pattern. Also during the silence, congregants may write brief prayers
on the distributed slips of paper. These will be brought forward as a burnt
offering during the Prayers of the People.)*

Hymn of Response   "Be Still, My Soul" (FINLANDIA)

The Time of Peace

Please greet one another with the peace of Christ.

LISTENING AND LETTING BE

Prayer for Illumination

Responsive Psalm   "On Eagles' Wings," Michael Joncas
(The people will join in singing the chorus/response as invited.)

Reading from the Hebrew Scriptures   Ecclesiastes 3:1–15

Reading from the New Testament   Revelation 21:1–5a

Sermon

The Response   "I Will Come to You (You Are Mine),"
David Haas

(An anthem, solo, or children's song, focusing on hope and peace, is also appropriate here.)

GOING FORTH IN HOPE, WITH PEACE

Affirmation of Faith

(Select an appropriate confessional statement from your tradition.)

Prayers of the People

These prayers are enacted. You are invited to come forward as you are able with your prayer slips *(of things written down earlier)* and light them afire, dropping them into a collection of deep buckets or pottery bowls. May our prayers—for forgiveness, for new beginnings, for courage, and for peace—ascend to God like an offering of incense.

Hymn   "God of the Sparrow" (ROEDER)

Blessing and Benediction

Postlude

Appendix 6
Additional Prayers and Litanies

CALLS TO WORSHIP
(Inspired by Psalm 25)

To you, O Lord, I lift up my soul.
O my God, in you I trust.
We do not know your ways, O Lord.
We do not know your paths.
Be mindful of your mercy, O Lord,
    and of your steadfast love,
    for they have been from old.
Turn to us and be gracious,
    for we are lonely and afflicted.
Relieve the troubles of our hearts,
    and bring us out of our distress.
Guard our life and deliver us.
We take refuge in you.
We await the redemption of our Lord.
Let us worship God!

or

We gather in the presence of a Holy and awesome God.
We gather with hearts broken and filled with sorrow.
We gather in the presence of a great cloud of witnesses.
We gather as a witness to pain and suffering.
We gather this day to worship the Risen Lord.
We gather this day to worship the Risen Lord.
Let us worship the Lord!

PRAYERS OF CONFESSION AND ASSURANCES OF PARDON

Prayer of Confession

God of comfort and assurance, we acknowledge our fear and our hurt and our worry. We pray for protection and yet have been touched by evil. We live with hope in the goodness of all, yet we see no goodness today. You are the God of life, and yet we gather to worship in the valley of the shadow of death. As we sit here, your people, gathered yet broken, forgive us for all that needs forgiving. Sit with us in the midst of our hurt and heartbreak. Guide us in the days ahead so that we might do your will, here on earth as it is in heaven. We ask this in Jesus' name. Amen.

Assurance of Pardon

Our God knows suffering and death. Our God knows heartache and hurt. Our God knows our pain. We are not alone. We are not forgotten. Suffering and death are not the end of our journey of faith. We believe in a God who calls forth new life out of death. We believe in a resurrected Lord who displaces fear with peace. We believe in a God who comforts all who mourn. Hear again the good news: the peace of God and the comfort of our Lord are with us now and forever. Amen.

Prayer of Confession after a Church Fire

God of goodness and mercy, we confess our hearts are broken today. Our beloved church building has been ravaged by fire—charred boards, ashes, that smell—a mess. Baptisms, weddings, funerals, meals shared together, praises lifted high, the Word proclaimed, your people forgiven, transformed, empowered and sent forth . . . and now this. We confess our grief, our dismay, our hurt. Our building has been destroyed, but our memories live on. Our church building has been burned, but our community of faith is together, strong, and whole. Forgive us for our sin. Continue to be with us as we assess, plan, rebuild, and move forward from this day. Guide us in all we do. Continue to bless us, the body of Christ, in this most special place. In Christ's name we pray. Amen.

Assurance of Pardon after a Church Fire

The Word of the Lord reminds us that when Jesus looked over Jerusalem, he wept. Surely, as God looks over us this day, God weeps with us. Fire has destroyed our beloved church building, yet the power and the presence of the Holy Spirit is alive within us all. We have not been abandoned. We will not be accursed. We will have our strength renewed, and we will mount up with wings like eagles. We will run and not be weary. We will walk and not faint, for the Lord, the everlasting God of goodness and grace, is with us now and forever and ever. Amen.

PASTORAL PRAYERS/PRAYERS OF THE PEOPLE

Gracious and loving God, we come to you with heavy and hurting hearts and ask that you hear our prayers. The events of the past (*days/hours*) have hurt us deeply—as individuals, as a community, and as the people of God gathered here. The violence that touched our congregation and our community has shocked and saddened us. We are filled to overflowing with tears and anger and questions and doubt. We want answers, but none are coming. We want healing, but it too must wait. We want to understand why, and yet we know, somewhere deep within, that we may never truly understand why. And so we turn to you, our rock and our redeemer, in a time like this—a time of hurt, and brokenness, and pain. We want the miracle of wholeness, but we know it will take time, a long time, to have the brokenness we feel in our hearts mended by your tender care.

We pray for _____ (*the victims, those affected*)

We pray for _____ (*all who responded*)

We pray for _____ (*others who have offered assistance*)

We pray for our community of faith (*name*), and all who serve in leadership.

(You may be tempted to insert here a prayer for the perpetrator, but in our experience, to name the person in worship does harm to an affected community of faith. Our advice is to not name the person, unless he/she/they were members of your congregation or staff. But again, this is tricky.)

We also pray for the events happening around us, mindful that while we have experienced this disaster of unimagined horror, life continues around us, among us, and through us.

We pray for _____ (*lift up ongoing concern for those in the congregation who are ill, needing prayer, etc.*)

We pray for _____ (*events in your community, country, the world. The idea here is to model placing the event in the context of the larger world and to remind folks that life is still moving forward around us.*)

Lord, we ask you to hear our prayer for all who suffer this day: for us, for those we've named, and for all the cares and concerns we carry within.

We also give you thanks and praise. We thank you this day for the opportunity to gather together as the body of Christ and offer you worship and praise, to lift our prayers to you, and to be reminded, yet again, of the mystery of your mercy and grace.

We thank you for the comfort and support of being together as a community of faith: to share stories, to hug and cry, to care for one another in ways that sustain and nurture us in our day-to-day living. Continue to be with us all as we go about our daily lives.

We also thank you for the good news of Jesus Christ, the resurrected Lord. We thank you for the promise of new life after death, even while we don't understand what that will mean for us. We thank you for the promise of peace, even while we continue to wrestle with fear and doubt, hurt and loss. We thank you for the assurance of being with us even, or especially, as we walk through this valley of the shadow of death. Be our comfort. Be our strength. Be with us now and forevermore. Amen.

Pastoral Prayer after a Violent Death

Gracious and Loving God, the unthinkable has occurred in our midst.
>   We have lost _____ (*name all those killed*), taken from us by _____ (*an accident, an act of violence, etc.*).
>   We are stricken with grief and unsure of what to do or say or even how to pray.
>   We want to cry out in rage. We want to cry out in sorrow.
>   We want to cry: Why have you forsaken us? Why did you let this happen to our beloved one(s) _____ (*name those killed*)?

We are hurting . . . (*long pause*) . . . and we are not sure of what to say.
We are angry. . . (*long pause*) . . . and we are not sure how to pray.
We are lost . . . (*long pause*) . . . and we are not sure we will ever find our way again.
We feel empty. . . (*long pause*) . . . and we wonder, will we ever feel okay?

Hear our prayers! Hear all of our prayers!
Hear us as we cry out to you in anguish.
Hear us as we cry out to you in rage.
Hear us as we cry out to you in grief.
Hear us as we simply cry.

Appendix 7
Praise Song and Contemporary Music Suggestions

"Amazing Grace/My Chains Are Gone" by Chris Tomlin

"Still" by Reuben Morgan

"Healing Is in Your Hands" by Chris Tomlin, Christy Nockels, Daniel Carson, Matt Redman, Nathan Nockels

"Oceans (Where Feet May Fail)" by Joel Houston, Matt Crocker, Salomon Lighthelm

"10,000 Reasons" by Matt Redman

"Blessings" by Laura Story

"Healing Rain" by Michael W. Smith

"Angel by Your Side" by Francesca Battistelli

"Word of God Speak" by Bart Millard, Pete Kipley

"Rescue" by Jared Anderson

"In Christ Alone" by Keith Getty, Stuart Townend

"More Love, More Power" by Jude Del Hierro

"Even When It Hurts" by Joel Houston

"That Where I Am" by Rich Mullins

When Grief Is Raw: Songs for Times of Sorrow and Bereavement, a collection by John L. Bell and Graham Maule, the Iona Community. Chicago: GIA Publications, Inc., 1997

Notes

Introduction

1. Shelly Rambo, *Spirit and Trauma: A Theology of Remaining* (Louisville, KY: Westminster John Knox Press, 2010), 8.

2. Robert Frost, "A Servant to Servants," in *The Poetry of Robert Frost*, ed. Edward Connery Lathem (New York: Holt, Rinehart and Winston, 1969), 64.

Chapter 2: Worship and Theology after Trauma

1. The Taizé Community is an ecumenical community founded in 1940 in the Burgundy region of France. Its worship is participative and global in nature, with music characterized by short, accessible tunes with simple texts in repetition, sung in a meditative manner.

2. Walter Brueggemann, *The Message of the Psalms* (Minneapolis: Augsburg Press, 1985), 20 (italics original).

3. Ibid., 52–53.

4. Job 23:2–9, *Tanakh: The Holy Scriptures* (New York: The Jewish Publication Society, 1985), 1372.

5. Walter Brueggemann, *Cadences of Home: Preaching among Exiles* (Louisville, KY: Westminster John Knox, 1997), 13 (italics original).

Chapter 3: Transitions

1. John Milton, "When I consider how my light is spent," in *The Poem: An Anthology, 2nd Edition,* ed. Stanley B. Greenfield and A. Kingsley Weatherhead (New York: Meredith Corporation, 1985), 119.

Chapter 4: Phase Two: Disillusionment

1. See further discussion on pp. 32–33.

2. Laurie Kraus's notes from trauma workshop for mental health practitioners, Louisville, KY, March 2013.

Chapter 5: Worship and Wondering in the Wilderness

1. Howard W. Polsky and Yaella Wozner, *Everyday Miracles: The Healing Wisdom of Hasidic Stories* (Northvale, NJ: Jason Aronson, Inc., 1989), 393.

2. Elie Wiesel, *Four Hasidic Masters and Their Struggle against Melancholy* (Notre Dame: University of Notre Dame Press, 1978), 60.

3. Mark Greiner, "Apocalypse and Recovery," in *Out of the Depths: Voices of the Presbyterian Faith Community at Work after September 11*, ed. Laurie Kraus (Louisville, KY: The Presbyterian Church (U.S.A.), 2002), 23–24.

4. Ibid.

5. Meister Eckhart, Meister Eckhart Quotes, Goodreads, accessed September 8, 2016, https://www.goodreads.com/author/quotes/73092; quoted in Evelyn Underhill, *Mysticism: A Study in the Nature and Development of Spiritual Consciousness* (1930; repr., Mineola, NY: Dover Publications, 2002), 305.

6. Fred Craddock, *Luke*, Interpretation: A Bible Commentary for Teaching and Preaching (Louisville, KY: John Knox Press, 1980), 287.

7. The Iona Community is an ecumenical Christian community committed to social justice and peace, established in 1938 on the island of Iona, Scotland. Iona has a vibrant contemporary worship and music practice in the Celtic tradition.

8. Dirk Lange, *Trauma Recalled: Liturgy, Disruption, and Theology* (Minneapolis: Fortress Press, 2010), 5, 10, 11.

Chapter 6: Phase Three: Reforming toward Wisdom

1. The Rev. Matthew Crebbin, as heard by Bruce Wismer.

2. The Rev. Dr. Bruce Wismer, committee meeting, Pine Shores Presbyterian Church, Sarasota, Florida, December 2013.

3. Robin Morgan, "Easter Island: I Embarkation," in *Lady of the Beasts: Poems* (New York: Random House, 1976), 43.

4. Walter Brueggemann, *The Message of the Psalms* (Minneapolis: Augsburg Press, 1985), 20 (italics original).

5. Ibid., 20–21.

Chapter 7: Phase Four: Wisdom

1. Julian of Norwich as quoted in Dan Graves, "Article #31: All Shall Be Well," {in context} The Stories behind Memorable Sayings in Church History, accessed September 8, 2016, https://www.christianhistoryinstitute.org/incontext/article/julian/.

2. Mary Oliver, "In the Storm," in *Thirst* (Boston: Beacon Press, 2006), 63.

Appendix 3: Vesper and Community Vigil Services

1. Julian of Norwich as quoted in Dan Graves, "Article #31: All Shall Be Well," {in context}: The Stories behind Memorable Sayings in Church History, accessed September 8, 2016, https://www.christianhistoryinstitute.org/incontext/article/julian/.

2. Saint Augustine of Hippo, *Confessions of a Sinner*, trans. R. S. Pine-Coffin (1961; repr., London: Penguin Books, 2004), 34–35.

Suggested Readings

Clergy Care

Day, Jackson, et al. *Risking Connection in Faith Communities: A Training Curriculum for Faith Leaders Supporting Trauma*. Brooklandville, MD: Sidran Institute, 2006.

Hunsinger, Deborah van Deusen. *Bearing the Unbearable: Trauma, Gospel, and Pastoral Care*. Grand Rapids, MI: Eerdmans, 2015.

Jones, Kirk Byron. *Rest in the Storm: Self-Care Strategies for Clergy and Other Caregivers*. Valley Forge, PA: Judson Press, 2001.

Richardson, Ronald W. *Becoming a Healthier Pastor: Creative Pastoral Care and Counseling*. Minneapolis: Fortress, 2004.

Rothschild, B. *Help for the Helper: The Psychophysiology of Compassion Fatigue and Vicarious Trauma, Self-Care Strategies for Managing Burnout and Stress*. New York: W. W. Norton, 2006.

Congregational Care

Aten, Jamie D., and David M. Boan. *Disaster Ministry Handbook*. Downers Grove, IL: Intervarsity, 2015.

Brener, Anne. *Mourning & Mitzvah: A Guided Journal for Walking the Mourner's Path through Grief to Healing*. Woodstock, VT: Jewish Lights Publishing, 2001.

Capps, Donald. *Agents of Hope: A Pastoral Psychology*. Eugene, OR: Wipf & Stock, 2001.

Hamman, J. J. *When Steeples Cry: Leading Congregations Through Loss and Change*. Cleveland: Pilgrim, 2005.

Haueisen, Kathryn M., and Carol Flores. *A Ready Hope: Effective Disaster Ministry for Congregations*. Herndon, VA: The Alban Institute, 2009.

Hunt, Gregory. *Leading Congregations through Crisis*. St. Louis: Chalice Press, 2012.

Roberts, Rabbi Stephen B., and the Rev. Willard W. C. Ashley Sr. *Disaster Spiritual Care: Practical Clergy Responses to Community, Regional, and National Tragedy*. Woodstock, VT: Skylight Paths, 2008.

Urquhart, George O'Neil. *Crisis and Emergency Management and Preparedness for the African-American Church Community: Biblical Applications from a Theological Perspective*. Eugene, OR: Wipf & Stock, 2014.

Biblical Interpretation, Worship, and Congregational Ministries

Brueggemann, Walter. *Praying the Psalms: Engaging Scripture and the Life of the Spirit.* 2nd ed. Eugene, OR: Wipf & Stock, 2007.

Moss, Otis, III. *Blue Note Preaching in a Post-Soul World: Finding Hope in the Midst of Despair.* Louisville, KY: Westminster John Knox, 2007.

O'Connor, Kathleen. *Jeremiah: Pain and Promise.* Minneapolis: Fortress, 2012.

———. *Job: New Collegeville Bible Commentary.* Collegeville, MN: Order of Saint Benedict, 2012.

———. *Lamentations and the Tears of the World.* Maryknoll, NY: Orbis, 2002.

Smith, Kathleen. *Stilling the Storm: Worship and Congregational Leadership in Difficult Times.* Herndon, VA: Alban, 2006.

Tamez, Elsa. *When the Horizons Close: Rereading Ecclesiastes.* Maryknoll, NY: Orbis, 2000.

Theology

Holcomb, Justin, and Lindsey Holcomb. *God Made All of Me.* Greensboro, NC: New Growth Press, 2015.

Jones, Serene. *Trauma and Grace: Theology in a Ruptured World.* Louisville, KY: Westminster John Knox, 2009.

Miller-McLemore, B. *In the Midst of Chaos: Caring for Children as Spiritual Practice.* San Francisco: Jossey-Bass, 2007.

Nouwen, Henri J. M. *The Return of the Prodigal Son.* New York: Image Books, Doubleday, 1992.

Rambo, Shelly. *Spirit and Trauma: A Theology of Remaining.* Louisville, KY: Westminster John Knox, 2010.

Trauma Understanding and Treatment—For Adults

Allen, J. G. *Coping with Trauma: Hope through Understanding.* Washington, DC: American Psychiatric Publications, 2005.

Baranowsky, Anna B., J. Eric Gentry, and D. F. Schultz. *Trauma Practice: Tools for Stabilization and Recovery.* New York: Huber & Hogrefe, 2005.

Catherall, Don R. *Handbook of Stress, Trauma, and the Family.* New York: Brunner-Routledge, 2004.

Cori, Jasmin Lee. *Healing from Trauma: A Survivor's Guide to Understanding Your Symptoms and Reclaiming Your Life.* Cambridge, MA: Da Capo Press, 2008.

Figley, C. R., ed. *Treating Compassion Fatigue.* New York: Routledge, 2002.

Levine, Peter A. *In an Unspoken Voice: How the Body Releases Trauma and Restores Goodness.* Foreword by Judith Herman and afterword by B. van der Kolk. Berkeley: North Atlantic Books, 2010.

O'Hanlon, Bill. *Quick Steps to Resolving Trauma.* New York: W. W. Norton, 2011.

Rothschild, B. *The Body Remembers: The Psychophysiology of Trauma and Trauma Treatment.* New York: W. W. Norton, 2000.

———. *8 Keys to Safe Trauma Recovery: Take-Charge Strategies to Empower Your Healing.* New York: W. W. Norton, 2010.

Schaefer, Charles, and Frauke Schaefer. *Trauma and Resilience: A Handbook.* Ebook: Condeopress.org, 2013.

van der Kolk, Bessel. *The Body Keeps the Score: Brain, Mind, and Body in the Healing of Trauma.* New York: Viking, 2014.

Weingarten, Kaethe. *Common Shock: Witnessing Violence Every Day.* New York: New American Library, 2003.

Yoder, Carolyn. *The Little Book of Trauma Healing: When Violence Strikes and Community Security Is Threatened.* Intercourse, PA: Good Books, 2005.

Trauma Treatment—For Children and Youth

Borgman, Dean. *Hear My Story: Understanding the Cries of Troubled Youth.* Peabody, MA: Hendrickson, 2003.

Holcomb, Justin, and Lindsey Holcomb. *God Made All of Me.* Greensboro, NC: New Growth Press, 2015.

Straus, Susan Farber. *Healing Days: A Guide for Kids Who Have Experienced Trauma.* Washington, DC: Magination, 2013.

Zubenko, W., and J. A. Capozzol, eds. *Children and Disasters: A Practical Guide to Healing and Recovery.* New York: Oxford University Press, 2002.

Websites

Compassion Unlimited   http://www.compassionunlimited.com

This is the website of traumatologist and compassion fatigue expert J. Eric Gentry, PhD, with resources, courses, and information about forward-facing trauma treatment, trauma-informed care, and compassion fatigue and resilience.

Institute for Congregational Trauma and Growth   http://www.ictg.org

The Institute for Congregational Trauma and Growth is a one-stop shop for congregation leaders to get latest information and training for trauma treatment among congregations and best practices for trauma-informed ministry.

Presbyterian Disaster Assistance   http://pda.pcusa.org

The website of Presbyterian Disaster Assistance, with resources and information on human-caused disaster responses, congregational and judicatory leadership support, and resources for worship after trauma and disaster.

On Clergy Sexual Misconduct

Gaede, B. A. *When a Congregation Is Betrayed: Responding to Clergy Misconduct.* Herndon, VA: The Alban Institute, 2005.

Horst, E. A. *Questions and Answers about Clergy Sexual Misconduct.* Collegeville, MN: The Liturgical Press, 2000.

Poling, J. N. *Understanding Male Violence: Pastoral Care Issues.* St. Louis: Chalice, 2003.

Waterstradt, Carolyn. *Fighting the Good Fight: Healing and Advocacy after Clergy Sexual Assault.* splatteredinkpress.com, 2012.

Websites

FaithTrust Institute   http://www.faithtrustinstitute.org

FaithTrust Institute is a national, multifaith, multicultural training and education organization with global reach working to end sexual and domestic violence.

GRACE   http://www.netgrace.org/

GRACE (Godly Response to Abuse in the Christian Environment) empowers and trains Christian communities to recognize, prevent, and respond to child abuse.

ISTI   http://www.saintjohnsabbey.org/interfaith-sexual-trauma-institute/

ISTI (Interfaith Sexual Trauma Institute) offers a lengthy list of organizations that can be utilized by victims of sexual abuse or exploitation. It also provides a bibliography of references, book reviews, publications, and a list of treatment programs and victims associations. ISTI conducts workshops and conferences.

Jewish Institute Supporting an Abuse-Free Environment   http://www.jsafe.org

The Jewish institute is an organization created to ensure and promote integrity within the Jewish community. The mission of JSafe is to create an environment in which every institution and organization across the entire spectrum of the Jewish community conducts itself responsibly and effectively in addressing the wrongs of domestic violence, child abuse, and professional improprieties— whenever and by whomever they are perpetrated.

The Hope of Survivors   http://www.thehopeofsurvivors.com

The Hope of Survivors is a nonprofit organization dedicated to assisting victims of pastoral sexual abuse and misconduct, as well as providing educational and informational materials and seminars to pastors and churches of every denomination, worldwide.

CPSIA information can be obtained
at www.ICGtesting.com
Printed in the USA
LVOW11s0049160317
527399LV00003B/408/P